MANAGEMENT ENRICHMENT TRAINING PROGRAM

MERIT sm

Written by: Jack Ferreri
Produced by: Linda Ewing
Edited by: Karen Storlie
Graphics by: Jack Ferreri
Center for Professional Development
Credit Union National Association, Inc.

ISBN 0-8403-7330-9

Printed in the United States of America
10 9 8 7 6 5 4 3

RECRUITING, INTERVIEWING AND SELECTING EMPLOYEES

KENDALL/HUNT PUBLISHING COMPANY
4050 Westmark Drive   Dubuque, Iowa 52002

ISBN 0-8403-7330-9

TABLE OF CONTENTS

Editor's Note: Since there is no singular pronoun that refers to both male and female, we mix the use of the generic "he" and "she" throughout this module. We acknowledge that many key managerial positions throughout the credit union movement are held by both men and women.

MERIT modules are designed to benefit not only managers, but up and coming supervisors as well as those striving for supervisory positions. You may notice that the terms supervisor and manager have been used interchangeably throughout this module. Some organizations carry manager titles for all employees overseeing staff. Other larger, organizations have many more staff levels and will often carry titles such as team leader, supervisor, manager, and director.

This module is not intended to provide any legal advice, nor do we guarantee that the information is accurate or valid for all state chartered credit unions. If you have any legal or policy questions, contact your credit union president or manager.

Acknowledgements

I would like to thank the following credit union professionals for their reviews of the manuscript.

Ted Fleagle, Colorado Credit Union Financial and Support System

Jerry Wolcott, Oregon Credit Union League

Dan Fisher, North Carolina Credit Union Network

Caryn Smola, Indiana Credit Union League

Nancy Pierce, Federal Employees Union, Kansas City

Maureen Hughes, Missouri Credit Union System

I would also like to thank the following groups for providing a number of sample forms and documents.

Carolyn Tadder, Center for Professional Development, CUNA, Inc.

Oregon Credit Union League

About the Author

Jack Ferreri is a professional free lance writer based in Verona, Wisconsin. He has taught at the university level, managed his own communications firm for several years, and has produced training and promotional materials since 1977.

Preface

Management Enrichment Training Program

The MERIT program is divided into two areas. The first area contains six courses that are considered basic and include the responsibilities that supervisors and managers are faced with on a day-to-day basis. The diagram below includes the titles of these first six courses. The second area will include, as they are developed, optional courses that supervisors and managers can pick and choose from to enhance their learning in particular areas of interest. These modules will greatly enhance job performance but may not be a job related requirement (for example: courses in team building, time management, and politics and the art of negotiation).

In order to be eligible for the first level MERIT certificate and lapel pin, you must successfully complete all six modules in the first area of the program. You become eligible for more advanced levels of certification with the completion of each additional six courses.

About This Module

This is one of the required modules in the first program area. This module must be completed as part of the requirements to receive your first level certificate and pin.

How To Use This Module

If you are sight impaired, you may choose to have this module read to you. A spouse, friend, or volunteer from your credit union or credit union league may assist you. Check with your local library regarding reader services available in your area.

If you are participating in a workshop or seminar, your instructor will give you your instructions. If you are taking this module through correspondence study:

1. Read the objectives located at the beginning of each chapter to get a good grasp of the material to come.
2. Read the module.
3. Complete exercises as you go

Management Enrichment Training Program

Required

M01   Fundamentals of Management
M02   Business Communications
M03   Recruiting, Interviewing, and Selecting Employees
M04   Training and Orienting Employees
M05   Delegating for Results
M06   Managing Employee Performance

Optional

M07   Managing Teamwork
M08   Process Improvement: Achieving Quality Together
M09   Developing Exceptional Leadership
       (Available Second Quarter 1995)
M10   Strategic Thinking and Planning
       (Available Fourth Quarter 1995)
M11   Compensation Systems *(Available Third Quarter 1995)*
M12   Workplace Diversity *(Available Third Quarter 1995)*

---

through the module. Once your exercises are completed, you can refer to the back of the module for answers (answers will not be provided for exercises designed for the individual reader).

4. When you are satisfied that you have mastered the material covered in this module, you are ready to take the competency test. Follow the instructions on the next page for completing your competency test.

5. Complete the course assessment form located at the back of the module. Send it with your test answers to your credit union league.

Competency Test Instructions

Each module in the Management Enrichment Training Program has a competency test. Each competency test has 40 multiple choice questions. To pass, you must correctly answer 32 or more questions.

All tests are open book. you can refer to the book to help answer the questions.

Tests are to be completed individually—without any other assistance than the book.

Directions

If you are participating in a conference or seminar, your instructor will give you instructions. If you are taking this module through correspondence study:

1. Your competency test will be mailed to you along with this module.

2. Recruit someone to monitor you while you take the test. Your monitor could be a spouse, friend, or a credit union employee who will be able to confirm that you did, in fact, complete the test alone. Your monitor will be required to also sign your test.

3. Find a quiet place where you can work undisturbed to complete the test.

4. You can use the book to help answer the questions.

5. Take as much time as you need. There is no time limit.

6. Complete the identification section (name, address, etc.). Follow the instructions on the test for marking your answers to the multiple choice questions.

7. When you have completed the test, make sure all your identification information is complete and you have marked an answer for each question. Sign the test and have your monitor sign the test.

8. Mail the completed test (questions and answers) to the address listed on the test.

Introduction

When it's time for you to hire new employees, you face special demands. Bringing new people into an existing work environment can be a challenging task. Every manager has faced the loss of a valued employee, and the prospect of replacing that person from a world of strangers.

We all know hiring people to fill a job opening is far from an objective decision. There's no *Consumer's Digest* to provide scientific first-hand evaluations of people, no definitive standard against which to measure our impressions.

In spite of the ways we try to formalize it, hiring people remains a subjective decision. And the hirer's purely personal preference doesn't provide much assurance in hiring a good credit union employee. Unfortunately, there is no better instrument for hiring people than a sharp manager who has learned from his or her mistakes and successes. The purpose of this manual is to give you some basic skills in recruiting, interviewing, and hiring.

How well you recruit reflects on your skills as a manager. The adept manager has a plan for hiring. Why? Because he must be ready to bring a new person on board quickly. Credit unions are never overstaffed, so the departure of an employee leaves you with a service gap to fill, which strains your operations and may have a negative effect on the service you provide to your members.

As a manager, you know the importance of good screening of job applicants. Not only must they have the skills to perform the job, but they must have the people skills to work with members, as well as with your existing team. Members interact with front-line workers more often than with any other credit union staff.

As a manager, you know the importance of good screening of job applicants. Not only must they have the skills to perform the job, but they must have the people skills to work with members, as well as with your existing team.

In addition to looking for job and people skills, it's also important for you to remember another aspect of job screening: the legal side of hiring.

Any hiring you do must take place in a legal environment. Several forces over the last three decades have led to the formulation of specific governmental guidelines on the ways you may go about recruiting, the types of questions you may ask, and the overall composition of your workforce. Hiring without an understanding of this environment leaves you open to lawsuits from unhappy applicants and employees, as well as charges of insensitivity from your community. The

INTRODUCTION

legal framework of employment decisions dictates you must familiarize yourself with applicable state and federal regulations. It is helpful to have an attorney on staff or on call to help with hiring issues.

If you absorb the material covered in this manual, you will be able to use some proven techniques to boost your hiring success rate and hire new people with more confidence.

This manual is designed to give you a set of skills which can help you obtain good results in your search to fill an employment position. You will learn how to:

- Actively recruit people who will do a good job for you.
- Evaluate those people and conduct a productive, informative, and legal job interview.
- Evaluate the results of your search and analysis, and to make the best hiring decisions.

Chapter One: Starting the Hiring Process

So you have a job opening. Maybe one of your employees left. Or you have created a new position to ease the workload in one of your harried departments. One way or another, you have a slot to fill. Candidates? Well, the United States population over age 18 is now about 172,000,000, yourself included. Your task is to decide how best to make one of those people—just one—a co-worker—a productive and smoothly-functioning member of your credit union. It shouldn't be too hard, should it?

The Classic Hiring Pitfalls

Before introducing you to the hiring process, it's important to note some common tendencies managers naturally fall into without realizing the impact. Please keep these in mind when hiring.

- **Insecure managers hire weak people.** It's a natural human tendency to want to stay on top of the hill, to bring people into the organization that won't challenge us. Some managers hire only safe people, those who satisfy the minimum requirements of the job, but lack any of the dynamic spark that might make a top-notch employee, the employee destined to go somewhere. This very human failing can lead to a work-

Objectives

> **Upon completion of this chapter, you will be able to:**
> 1. **Conduct an exit interview.**
> 2. **Update and reassess existing job descriptions.**
> 3. **Analyze a job in the specific skills required.**
> 4. **Help to establish realistic salary levels.**
> 5. **Be able to explain your credit union's benefit package.**

place riddled with mediocrity. The surest way to win recognition for yourself and for your organization is to bring in the strongest employees you can find. No professional sports coach ever won a championship by passing up the most skilled players.

- **Managers hire themselves.** Most of us are hung up on our own values. So we hire like we vote; we select people that resemble us. In general, we like ourselves, and we have some trouble understanding why anyone would want to be different from us. So when we bring people on board to work for us, we want dependable, serious-minded, upright people—just like us. If you are charged with hiring people, you must look beyond

So when we bring people on board to work for us, we want dependable, serious-minded, upright people—just like us.

your particular strengths, and bring in other talents and abilities, sometimes very different from your own.

In agriculture, when you have planted a field with just a single crop hybrid, you have a field that's all of one height, ripening at one time, and of a single level of quality. That has its benefits. But experts point out a danger. If everyone in an area plants the same kind of crop, a terrible vulnerability emerges. Suppose a virus or insect pest comes along that's particularly well-adapted to destroying this hybrid crop. Without diversity, all area crops would perish. A mix of different hybrids on different fields would provide strength through diversity. Not all hybrids will be vulnerable to a single attacker.

It's the same diversification message financial planners preach to their clients. If you spread your risk across a wide assortment of financial vehicles—stocks, bonds, real estate, cash, gold—you are less likely to confront serious trouble.

How this diversity applies to your hiring practices should be obvious. A credit union full of matching personalities is not a healthy financial institution. You need one sort of person to handle receptionist duty in the lobby, someone out-going, friendly, a real people person. For the back office, you want different qualities—attention to detail, thoroughness, persistence. Supervisors need a combination of both talents. Imagine a credit union made up wholly of suspicious people or trusting people, of aggressive people or shy people.

Diversity gives you the best chance to utilize complementary talents. A rich combination of different skills will produce the best results.

- **Managers hire people that are more over-qualified than under-qualified.** Managers talk a great deal about finding people who have the minimum qualifications they need. But the fact is a far greater percentage of people will leave because they're over-qualified for a job, rather than under-qualified. We all want competence in our new employees, but we must be realistic in matching person to position. Hiring a college graduate as a night security guard isn't a bargain; it is a poor match that will likely need to be undone in a short time. People have a greater capacity for being challenged than for being bored.

- **Managers will make the "safe" hire.** In the microcomputer world, it is said that "no one was ever fired for buying IBM." In the confusing technical world of computer purchasing, buyers may pass up a better value with an unknown product by playing safe with the market's front runner. They go with the brand name because, if a problem emerges, the boss can never say, "Yeah, but Jones, there, brought in this risky computer system and look where it's left us!" In the world of hiring, managers tend to be conservative in evaluating job candidates.

Prudence is good, but it can be carried to extremes. Sometimes you will be able to land a better prospect by letting your instincts and insight guide your decision. Your "gamble" must still meet the basic job requirements, of course.

- **Managers look outside to hire, without considering the existing employee pool.** Too often, we automatically go outside our organization to fill vacancies. Sometimes that's necessary, of course, but inside hiring offers many solid advantages. We detail those advantages in chapter two. You should keep the in-house labor market in mind at all times, especially in a service industry, where personal contact and involvement are so important. Sometimes the grass *isn't* greener on the other side.

Taking a Systematic Approach

Bringing a new person into your organization, or promoting a current employee to a new job, demands a systematic approach.

Activity 1.1

Test your objectivity by considering your friends as job applicants. Review the following much-abbreviated job description.

Administrative Assistant

- 40 hours per week
- must be familiar with business environment
- must type 50 words per minute
- must be familiar with word processing software
- must have strong people skills
- must coordinate reports from several departments for submission to senior management

List four people you know *outside your work* and evaluate them as candidates for this position. Look at their skills objectively and evaluate them in each of the listed categories. Fill in all blanks. Which one would you hire for the job?

Name	Skill	Possesses Skill (1=low to 10=high)	Hiring Choice
_____	work 40 hours	_____	_____
_____	type 50 wpm	_____	_____
_____	word processing	_____	_____
_____	people skills	_____	_____
_____	coordination	_____	_____

This isn't something you should plan to do without careful thought and laying down some groundwork. If you can't spend the equivalent of at least two full days assessing the position, defining the qualifications, recruiting the applicants, conducting an initial screening, interviewing, and making your final decision, then you are not serious enough about hiring the best person for the job.

There's another issue in being organized for hiring. You should keep yourself ready *at all times* to undertake a quick job search. People leave their jobs for all sorts of reasons. The most com-

Figure 1.1 Sample Credit Union Policy on Job Openings, Recruitment and Selection

I. POLICY

It is the policy of the credit union to be an equal opportunity employer and to hire individuals solely upon the basics of qualifications for the job to be filled. Unless otherwise provided in writing and signed by the__P__, employment with the credit union is considered to be at-will, so that either party may terminate the relationship at any time.

II. GUIDELINES

A. Managers who need to fill a job opening or want to add a new job position should submit a request in writing to the__P__for approval. Managers are to follow all the appropriate policy guidelines as outlined in the Employment section of this policy manual (i.e., the 300 policy series) when filling all open positions.

B. The credit union will normally try to fill job openings by promoting from within if qualified applicants are available internally. Managers reviewing internal applicants for transfer may request only the following from the employee's personnel file: application, performance appraisals, disciplinary records, reference information, and attendance/tardiness records.

C. Candidates from within the credit union will be reviewed and processed as outlined in the Promotion, Transfer & Demotion Policy.

D. Any external candidate for employment must fill out and sign an employment application form in order to be considered for hiring. Applications are to be maintained on file for__M__months.

E. A former terminated employee who is re-employed will be considered a new employee from the date of re-employment unless the break in service is less than thirty days, in which case the employee will retain accumulated seniority. Length of service for the purpose of benefits is governed by the terms of each benefit plan. Employees who retire may be eligible, in certain circumstances to be considered for rehire.

F. During the selection process, managers should follow these guidelines:
1. No notes or comments are to be made on the application form itself. Any notes or comments should be made on a *separate* sheet of paper.
2. Managers should describe the job to be filled as clearly as possible and show the applicant a copy of the job description. Hours of work, salary range, benefits and an overview of the department and credit union should also be covered.
3. All employment is subject to the receipt of acceptable references and eligibility to work in the U.S. Verification as to their backgrounds in employment, education, bonding and credit should be made. Whenever a credit record plays a role in an applicant's rejection, they must be advised of this fact and also informed as to the source of the negative information.
4. Manager must obtain approval from the__P__on the candidate selected and salary recommended before extending a formal offer.

Figure 1.1 Sample Credit Union Policy on Job Openings, Recruitment and Selection   *page 2*

> 5. Once a formal offer has been offered, the managers should verify the employee selected is legal to work in the United States by having them complete the Federal I-9 Form and initiate bonding procedures.
> 6. Manager will extend a written offer of employment which should include the job title, bi-monthly salary, hours of work, a contract disclaimer, and other pertinent information.
>
> G. Once the position has been filled, other applicants should be promptly notified. The response to these applicants should be "THANK YOU FOR YOUR INTEREST IN... WE HAVE SELECTED THE APPLICANT THAT IN OUR OPINION BEST MATCHED THE POSITION." No other information should be given on the selection process with the *exception* of negative credit reports as mentioned above. This standard response should be given when applicants ask "why" they were not chosen to avoid possible legal liabilities.
>
> H. Legal Issues
>
> Discrimination charges can be filed by individuals who feel they have been denied a job because of membership in a protected employment classification. When interviewing candidates, it is essential to avoid any form of illegal discrimination, intentional or unintentional. Unintentional discrimination is just as illegal as intentional discrimination. Managers must be aware of areas in which even apparently innocent questions, asked in good faith, can leave the credit union and the interviewer open to costly charges of discrimination. Seventy percent of discrimination complaints have occurred as the result of the interviewing process. Examples of specific interviewing questions are shown on the attached.
>
> Attachment: Guidelines for Conducting Non-Discriminatory Interview
>
> **OPTIONS & REMINDERS**
>
> Option:
>
> 01 _____ A member of an employee's family (by blood or marriage) will not be hired into a position or supervised by a family member except in cases of non-regular employment for a limited duration.

Figure 1.1 Sample Credit Union Policy on Job Openings, Recruitment and Selection   *page 3*

GUIDELINES FOR CONDUCTING NON-DISCRIMINATORY INTERVIEWS

Subject:

Name

Lawful Inquiries: Is any additional information relative to change of name, use of an assumed name, or nickname necessary to enable a check on your work record? If yes, explain.

Unlawful Inquiries: What is your original name? (Applicant whose name has been changed by court order or otherwise; or maiden name of a married woman) Have you ever worked under another name?

Marital & Family Status

Lawful Inquiries: Can you meet specified work schedules? Do you have activities, commitments or responsibilities that may hinder the meeting of work attendance requirements?

Unlawful Inquiries: Are you married, single, divorced, engaged, etc.? How many children do you have? What are their ages? Are you pregnant? Do you plan on having a family? (Any such questions which directly or indirectly might result in limitation of job opportunity in any way. If an applicant is pregnant she cannot be denied the job just because she is pregnant.) What are your marriage plans? What does your spouse do? What happens if your spouse gets transferred or needs to relocate? Who will take care of your child while you are at work?

References

Lawful: By whom were you referred for a position here? Can you give me the names of persons willing to provide professional and/or character references for you? Who suggested that you apply for a position here?

Unlawful: Require the submission of a religious reference. Request reference from applicant's pastor.

Age

Lawful: Are you under the age of 18?

Unlawful: How old are you? What is your date of birth? How would you feel working for a person younger than you?

Sex

Lawful: No questions should be asked relating to this subject.

Unlawful: A pre-employment inquiry as to sex on an application form shall be unlawful Do not ask a man how he would feel working for a woman or vice versa.

Race or Color

Lawful: No questions should be asked relating to this subject.

Unlawful: Complexion or color of skin. Coloring. Do you feel that your sex/race/color will be a problem in you performing your job?

Ancestry or National Origin

Lawful: What languages do you read, speak or write fluently?

Unlawful: What is your lineage, ancestry, national origin, descent, birthplace, or mother tongue? What is the national origin of parents or spouse?

Religion

Lawful: No questions should be asked relating to this subject.

Unlawful: What is your religious denomination, religious affiliations, church, parish, pastor, or religious holidays observed? An applicant may not be told, "This is a (Catholic, Protestant, or Jewish) organization." Do you hold any religious beliefs that would prevent you from working certain days of the week?

Figure 1.1 Sample Credit Union Policy on Job Openings, Recruitment and Selection   *page 4*

Address or Duration of Residence	**Lawful:** What is your address? How long a resident of this state or city? **Unlawful:** Specific inquiry into foreign addresses which would indicate national origin. What are the names or relationship of persons with whom you reside? Do you own or rent a home?
Military Record	**Lawful:** What education and experience did you have in the service that relates to the job you are interviewing for? **Unlawful:** What type of discharge did you receive? Did you receive a dishonorable discharge?
Education	**Lawful:** What academic, vocational or professional education and private or public schools have you attended? What is the highest grade you completed? **Unlawful:** Why did you attend? Did you receive loans or aids for education? How much? What year did you graduate from high school?
Character	**Lawful:** Have you ever been convicted of a crime? If so, when, where and what is the disposition of your offense? **Unlawful:** Have you ever been arrested? (An employer's use of an individual's arrest record to deny employment would, in the absence of business necessity, constitute a violation of the fair employment laws.)
Relatives	**Lawful:** Do you have any relatives already employed by us? **Unlawful:** What are the names, addresses, ages, number or other information concerning applicant's children or other relatives not employed by the company.
Credit Rating	**Lawful:** Nothing unless specific business requirements can be shown. When specifically job-related circumstances apply, indicate that a credit check will be done and ask if they will have any objections to this. Tell them they will be advised of any negative information which causes their rejection and the source of this information. **Unlawful:** Any questions concerning credit rating, charge accounts, etc. Not advising an applicant when a negative report contributes to their rejection. Refusing to divulge the source of negative credit information.

Figure 1.1 Sample Credit Union Policy on Job Openings, Recruitment and Selection   *page 5*

CREDIT UNION

SUBJECT: PROMOTION, DEMOTION AND TRANSFER

EFFECTIVE DATE: 11-1-91   **SUPERSEDES: 10-1-91**

I.   POLICY:

It is the policy of the credit union that it may at its discretion initiate or approve employee job transfers-from on job to another.

II. GUIDELINES:

A.   Job transfers are defined as promotions, demotions and lateral transfers. All personnel policies governing the credit union's employment practices apply to all internal transfers and should be followed by managers.

B.   Managers reviewing internal applicants for transfer may only request the following from the employee's personnel file: application, performance appraisals, disciplinary records, reference information, and attendance/ tardiness records.

C.   The credit union may require employees to make either a temporary or longterm job transfer in order to accommodate the organization's business needs.

D.   All promotions, demotions, transfers, and wage/salary changes must be approved in advance by the __P__

E.   All internal applicants not selected should be promptly notified. Managers should limit their response. as to WHY an applicant was not selected for the position to: "THANK YOU FOR YOUR INTEREST IN …WE HAVE SELECTED THE CANDIDATE THAT IN OUR OPINION BEST MATCHED THE POSITION." No further information on the selection process should be given when applicants ask "why" they were not chosen with the *exception* of negative credit reports. If a credit record played a role in the applicant's rejection, they must be advised of this fact and also informed as to the source of the negative information.

mon are marriage, parenting, and moving. A skilled manager prepares herself to replace people at any time. After all, you may have to find a new employee quickly if an existing worker must leave unexpectedly due to family events such as illness or relocation.

Additionally, you should stay ahead of the personnel game by periodically reviewing your staff. Do you need to add people due to increased member activity or a new service or branch? What are your strategic business trends? Will you be shifting people within different departments? A savvy manager will consider his or her alternatives.

In summary, be prepared with

A frank exit interview can often yield important information you can use when bringing in a replacement.

a plan of action for any departures or increased staffing needs. Just as your credit union has contingency plans for all sorts of things (fires, robberies, malfunctioning equipment), you should likewise develop a policy or procedure for bringing in new people. Figure 1.1 provides a sample policy for job openings, recruitment and selection from the Personnel Policy Manual for managers available through CUNA's HR Consulting Services and your league.

Activity 1.2

Prepare exit interview questions for the following situation.

Marianne Brady told you last week she'd be leaving her bookkeeping position at the end of the month. The reason she gave you for leaving was vague: "Personal reasons. I just want something that's more suited to me." You hired Marianne seven months ago.

Write down at least six questions you think would be proper to ask Marianne and which might lead you to learn how to do a better job of hiring next time.

1. _____

2. _____

3. _____

4. _____

5. _____

6. _____

_____

_____

_____

_____

The Exit Interview

The first step you should take is to decide why you have an opening. Why did the previous jobholder leave? This is especially significant in those positions that show a higher than normal turnover. The reasons may be obvious—perhaps the individual is leaving town, taking a better position, or going back to school. But more often the answer is not so simple.

A frank exit interview can often yield important information you can use when bringing in a replacement. After all, the person leaving may have nothing to lose by being totally honest. You can ask questions you might feel uncomfortable asking current employees. Perhaps the job is simply too demanding, or not demanding enough. Perhaps it requires too much responsibility for too little pay. You may find the person really didn't want to leave, but felt he had to due to personality conflicts with co-workers or supervisors. You will be more successful at replacement hiring when you really know *why* the departing employee left.

Experienced managers have found that sitting down with the departing employee, when that person has no reason *not* to tell you the truth, can be instructive. Develop a number of questions you can ask in this interview.

You should appreciate, however, that people leaving a job don't always know why they are leaving. Or they may think they're leaving for one reason and actually leaving for another. A sensitive interviewer can sometimes get at the cause of departure indirectly by careful questioning. If you ask a person what they like about the job they're going to, you can get a good sense of what they didn't like about the job they're leaving. Suppose, for example, a departing employee speaks excitedly about the healthy salary and the greater sense of responsibility the new job brings. You can be confident, then, that salary and overly-close supervision were elements in the departure.

Some managers suggest the immediate supervisor or manager should not do the exit interview. Of course, this depends on the personal situation and the credit union's personnel structure. If you have enough staff, it's best to assign the exit interview to professional human resource people. The direct supervisor or manager can still provide some suggested topics for discussion.

Figure 1.2 Sample Questions for an Exit Interview

- What parts of your job didn't you like?
- What parts of your job were the most satisfying?
- Were you worked too hard or not hard enough?
- Was your salary level satisfactory, or as satisfactory as salaries can ever be?
- What changes would you recommend in your job for the next person to hold your position?
- How were you treated by supervisors and managers in your time with us?
- Is there anything else we can do for you?
- Can I write you a letter of recommendation (if you feel this person's work truly was commendable)? How many copies would you like and when would you like them?

Determining the Type of Person that You Need

You should review job descriptions each time you're hiring for a position, and annually even if you don't rehire.

People come in all types. What kind do you need?

- A take-charge person who's goal-oriented and can work well unsupervised?
- A "numbers" person who will work for hours to find a missing twenty-five cents?
- A "people" person, someone who everyone likes and who can make everyone—staff and members alike—feel special?

Think of any situation comedy on television. These shows guarantee their success through the interplay of a carefully-selected ensemble of actors. The group consists of various sorts of characters who relate well, or at least entertainingly, together. Pick your sitcom—*The Mary Tyler Moore Show, All in the Family, The Andy Griffith Show, M.A.S.H., The Cosby Show, Murphy Brown, Designing Women*—they all present a rich cross-section of people we recognize, more or less, in real life. The more life experiences we have, the greater the number of people and different types of personalities we will run into. All this experience, we are told, will make us wiser.

People are all the adjectives you can think of: somber, vivacious, charismatic, energetic, dutiful, lackadaisical, intense, fun-loving. Some employees love

---

Activity 1.3
Match the job with the personality trait

Listed below are several jobs our society needs. Next to each write down a half-dozen personality traits you think would be most appropriate to the particular job.

Religious leader _____

Judge _____

Plumber _____

Accountant _____

Professional marathon runner _____

Dairy farmer _____

Hunting guide _____

Advertising executive _____

Special education teacher _____

Credit union teller _____

Loan officer _____

Answers for this activity are found in appendix A at the back of this manual.

working with people; others hate it. Some like to focus on situations where there is always one right answer, and the trick is to find it. Others are more comfortable with open-ended situations (like hiring employees), where there are no right or wrong answers, just shades of grey. When hiring for your credit union, one of the first questions you will need to address is what type of person the position requires.

People do best in those jobs that fit their personality type. For example, the ranks of firefighters are made up of men and women who enjoy physical challenges, prefer hands-on involvement in things, and aren't afraid of a little danger. Most attorneys are more likely to enjoy intellectual combat, and they're likely to take pleasure in details. Forgive the stereotypes for a minute, but imagine a librarian called on to fight a raging fire. Or imagine a firefighter asked to catalog a shipment of two hundred new book arrivals.

In summary, make a point of thinking about the type of personality you want in the person to fill your position. It will make a difference in how soon you'll have a vacancy in that slot again.

Reassessing the Job Description

If the job you're filling doesn't have a job description, write one. If the existing job description seems inadequate, but you're not sure how to put together a good one, try writing a description of your own job. You will learn things about putting together job descriptions, and about your own job, you didn't know before.

Some human resource managers refer to this review of the job description by a special name—job analysis. Some distinguish between job descriptions and job specifications. You can analyze it any way you want, but the fact remains you will need to be sure that the way you describe the job, detail by detail, is accurate. Small credit unions need better, more tightly written job descriptions. A small number of people must cover all the bases in a small financial institution. So each description must cover all aspects of the job. Tasks that fall between job descriptions aren't going to get done.

As of July 1991, even small credit unions (fifteen or more employees) must comply with the federal Americans with Disabilities Act. This legislation distinguishes between essential and non-essential functions of a position with respect to disabled applicants and employees.

You should do a thorough review of existing job descriptions for a new hire. Only in this way can you be sure of several things:

- You know exactly what job it is you're talking about. Each job description in your credit union must be clearly distinct.
- You know what skills are needed by the applicant. This is the checklist against which you will judge candidates for the position.
- That you can prove your hir-

ing standards are objective and unbiased. This is no small issue in the America of the 1990s, when your goodwill and fairness in hiring must be clearly provable.

You should review job descriptions each time you're hiring for a position, and annually even if you don't rehire. As we saw earlier, you can draw on your exit interview with the departing employee to refine and refocus the active job description. Another technique used by some managers is to consider the positions with which the new employee will interact. Does the job description accurately detail the nature of the interchange? Should the interaction be modified? In other words, should the holder of the job do more, less, or something different in interacting with the other positions or departments? This constant reality check will keep job descriptions truly useful.

Be warned, however, that some people want to push work off on others, while others look for more responsibility and advancement. If you are talking to someone who interacts with the person in the job you're reviewing, make sure he isn't responding to your questions based on his personal agenda.

One technique often recommended by management experts is management by walking around. This works equally well in reviewing job descriptions. Take some time over a week or two to see with your own eyes what the job position in question actually entails. Sometimes what's written on paper differs from what actually happens on the job. Keep notes on what you see over time and then review them prior to discussing the topic with the current jobholder, usually in the exit interview.

It's important you recognize that your goal here is not to find fault, just reality. Sometimes you will be surprised at just what makes up a particular job. We all tend to pigeon-hole employees. If someone's job title is clerk or teller or bookkeeper, we tend to think we know what makes up their job. That's not always true.

Money isn't the only reason for working, but it's generally the major one. Most of us, in one way or another, judge ourselves by the value with which society rewards our efforts.

Once you list all the skills you want your employee to have, it's time to get realistic. If the perfect employee doesn't show up for an interview, ask yourself which listed job skills would be nice to have and which skills are a must for the job. In a tight labor market, with a slim salary budget, you may have to go for the essentials. A car drives very well without an air conditioner, but without a transmission it goes nowhere. This principle can also be considered when looking at job applicants. For example, a customer service representative can perform nicely without being a mathematical genius. But without people skills, that representative can't perform well.

Your job description becomes the basis for hiring, evaluating, retraining, and possibly promoting the person holding the job.

Company-provided (for larger credit unions) or company-funded daycare is a hot topic in the nineties, with more and more two-earner families in the workforce.

You need to weigh this in formulating the description. It can easily become a legal document. If you have any doubts of this, speak to an attorney with experience in personnel matters.

Many job descriptions currently in use are inadequate. Figures 1.3 and 1.4 show sample job descriptions for the same job—a department secretary. The first one demonstrates the way a typical job description is written. The second enhances the responsibilities and is much more specific.

There are many resources you can draw on in putting together your job descriptions. These can be used to bring your credit union's job descriptions up-to-date, if needed. Samples of these job descriptions can be seen in figures 1.5 and 1.6. Figure 1.7 provides general guidelines for the contents of a complete job description.

Figure 1.8 is a position description worksheet for your use in creating job descriptions. You can use this worksheet for existing or new positions within your credit union. It can also be helpful during recruiting to review and summarize the position with the candidate during the interview.

How to Set a Salary

Part of what you will be doing each time you review a job description and each time you rehire for a position is to review the salary level. As your experience has already probably taught you, money can be a troublesome issue in the marketplace.

Most businesses take the safe course of keeping wages the same year to year, adding either merit adjustments or occasional cost of living increases. Often, additional increases or an occasional decrease in salary can spring from local employment conditions. For example, in the early 1990s our population shows a lower level of teenage workers available than in earlier years. This has led fast-food operations—a prime employer of unskilled young people—to find themselves in a bidding war with each other to draw workers. Many employers found themselves offering new hires a premium above minimum wage. They also set up monetary reward programs to compensate current employees for referring new workers to the operation.

Money isn't the only reason for working, but it's generally the major one. Most of us, in one way or another, judge ourselves by the value with which society rewards our efforts. The more money we make, the better we feel, since this tells us someone feels we're of considerable value. We all know personal fulfillment is also an important variable in worker satisfaction. Even a top-paid worker can feel dissatisfied in a job.

Research over the years has shown that workers are more sensitive to their wages compared with other workers on the job than they are to the absolute value of their take-home pay. In other words, if a worker sees that someone with considerably less experience and skill is making approximately the same salary, that will prove far more grating on the employee than any particular salary level. Employees want a fair salary—fair in the context of the people included in a particular workplace and a particular market. Put another way, if pay isn't a

Figure 1.3 Typical Job Description

Job Title:	Department Secretary
Responsibilities:	Works under the direction of the supervisor, Member Service Department
Duties:	• Types correspondence and reports • Compiles reports • Maintains inventory of supplies • Arranges meetings and conferences for the supervisor • Handles routine incoming correspondence • Answers phone and takes messages • Others as assigned
Qualifications:	• High school diploma or equivalent • 45 wpm typed • Two years experience in a secretarial position, or equivalent education

Figure 1.4 Enhanced Job Description

Job Title:	Department Secretary
Responsibilities:	Performs responsible, sometimes confidential, secretarial duties and routine administrative functions for the supervisor, Member Service Department
Duties:	• Types and proofreads reports, correspondence, forms, etc.; may type confidential materials; may use dictaphone or word processing equipment • Answers the telephone; takes and relays messages; responds to routine telephone inquiries; forwards calls to appropriate parties; maintains statistical information on number of incoming/outgoing calls • Prepares daily appointment schedule for supervisor; makes and confirms appointments as directed; schedules meetings and takes minutes as required • Organizes and maintains files of records and correspondence • Monitors departmental materials and supplies; orders as needed and verifies accuracy of supplies received • Maintains personnel and payroll records of a routine nature; may prepare employee work schedules
Qualifications:	• Working knowledge of business English, spelling, and arithmetic; office practices and procedures; operation of office equipment; basic principles of bookkeeping and of Lotus 1-2-3; may be required to type accurately at a speed of at least 45 words per minute • Ability to develop and maintain effective working relationships with co-workers; to be tactful in dealing with the general public; to prioritize assignments and organize work efficiently; and to handle routine administrative details; considerable skill in oral communication and in operating a word processor (DOS WordPerfect 5.1); some skill in operating personal computers; skill in shorthand desirable
Education and Experience:	• Knowledge, skill, and mental development equivalent to completion of four years of high school with courses in typing, business machine operation, and general office procedures; two years of responsible office experience, or an acceptable equivalent combination of education and experience

Figure 1.5 Branch Manager Job Description

_____ Credit Union

Position Description

Title: Branch Manager   Effective Date: _____
Department: Branch Operations   Grade: _____
Reports To: Assistant Manager   Status: Exempt
Supervises: Branch Staff
Approved By:

Primary Function

Responsible for the administration and supervision of all branch activities within established policies and guidelines.

Major Duties and Responsibilities

1. Direct, develop, motivate, hire, and discipline branch personnel.
2. Determine that all credit union policies are being followed and initiate corrective action as needed and directed by supervisor.
3. Review operational problems with staff and other department personnel for solutions or modifications to operations.
4. Work with loan manager in coordination and implementation of loan policy for branches.
5. Work with collection manager implementing branch collection efforts.
6. Recommend and develop innovative programs/services in which the credit union should participate.
7. Control branch office security.
8. Balance cash, general ledger, and daily reconciliation sheet daily.
9. Sign checks, and reconcile petty cash and replenish as necessary.
10. Supervise bond redemptions, signing up of new members, opening of share accounts, and purchasing of all types of certificates.
11. Resolve account problems and provide information to members.
12. Maintain liaison between branch office and main office.
13. Cross-sell credit union services.
14. Perform other duties as required.

Skills, Knowledge, and Experience

A college degree (prefer business or related major) or equivalent and a minimum of three to five years experience in the lending or member services area of a credit union or financial institution. Ability to make decisions and supervise subordinates effectively. Ability to communicate well with suborindates, associates, and members. Knowledge of managerial techniques, operations procedures, principles of lending and collections, marketing, and the credit union philosophy.

This position description is not a complete statement of all duties and responsibilities comprising your position. It contains only the facts necessary to evaluate your position on a fair basis.

Figure 1.6 Teller Job Description

_____ Credit Union

Position Description

Title: Teller
Department: Operations
Reports To: Chief Teller
Supervises: N/A
Approved By:

Effective Date: _____
Grade: _____
Status: Non-Exempt

Primary Function

Responsible for the accurate servicing of varied financial transactions for the membership.

Major Duties and Responsibilities

1. Receives and processes members' current financial transactions, including deposits, withdrawals, and loan payments. Sells money orders and travelers checks to members. Handles all member transfers via telephone.
2. Balances cash drawer and makes settlement of day's activities.
3. Welcomes members to the credit union and provides routine information concerning services in accordance with credit union policies. Directs members to the appropriate department for specific information and service.
4. Answers member inquiries and solves member problems regarding savings and loan programs, and other credit union services.
5. Cross-sells all services of the credit union which benefit the member.
6. Performs a variety of miscellaneous duties, including typing, filing, computer input, and telephone answering.
7. Performs other duties and responsibilities as assigned.

Skills, Knowledge, and Experience

Education equivalent to a high school degree plus specialized training in teller procedures. Considerable experience in cash handling and customer service is necessary. Ability to type work with numbers accurately, and use general office machines, including terminals. Knowledge of teller procedures, services for members, and credit union philosophy.

This position description is not a complete statement of all duties and responsibilities comprising your position. It contains only the facts necessary to evaluate your position on a fair basis.

true measure of performance, it doesn't keep good people on the job.

In looking at salary levels for your employees, recognize the six basic components of all compensation packages, from senior executives to maintenance workers:

- Base salary
- Vacation, sick, holiday, and incentive (if any) pay
- Insurance coverages (medical, dental, life)
- Pension/retirement plans (401K, Keogh, IRA)
- Other items (health club membership, childcare, parking, etc.)

As you develop your job description, you should also make a point to create a benefit chart or graph. This should depict the value of vacation time, along with potential sick time, insurance coverage value, and credit union contributions to pensions or retirement funds. In a competitive job market, the way you put together all of the job's benefits to the potential employee may well determine whether you get the quality level of employee you want. In a sense, you're marketing the job to the right employee.

You can determine the approximate standard for base pay in your geographic area by referring to *Credit Union Magazine's* "Complete Staff Compensation Survey" published every other year. Here you will see approximately what pay level is designated for each job in a typical credit union, based on geographic area and size of credit union. This is a starting point for determining base salary. Similarly, your Credit Union League, more local in nature than CUNA, Inc., may also prove helpful.

The competitive situation in your town or city will affect the way you establish salaries. Simple economics tells us that where there are many other job opportunities you will need to pay a little more to bring employees to you than in those situations (a buyer's market) in which

---

Figure 1.7 What Should a Complete Job Description Include?

- Job title, along with a representative salary range
- Benefits included with the job, including the starting time for the benefits
- List of essential and non-essential duties in considerable detail (the more general you are, the less valuable the job description)
- List of relevant performance standards of the job (for example, the teller should be handling between X and Y members a day, or the cash drawer should be balanced within X dollars/cents)
- List of positions or departments with which the worker will interact
- The position of the worker in the chain of command: who the worker reports to, and who reports to the worker
- Any equipment with which the worker should be familiar
- Any courses or special training the worker must have completed or will be required to complete
- Any experience requirements (for example, a head teller job description might specify that the individual must have at least four years of experience as a teller)
- Level of problem solving, interpersonal skills, and so on the job requires
- Possible career paths along which job holders might progress from this job
- Any training or initial review periods, including timing on initial job review and evaluation
- Whether the job includes any exposure to confidential or sensitive information
- The level of discretion, initiative, or independent judgment required

A standard worksheet for outlining the information required to complete a job description can be a useful tool for managers and supervisors. It also helps to ensure consistency of the documentation for whatever format the credit union has chosen to use. Figure 1.8 includes a sample Position Description Worksheet which you may copy for your own use.

Figure 1.8 Position Description Worksheet

Position Description

Position Title:_____ Grade: _____

Department: _____

Reports to (title): _____

Primary Function:

Education:

Experience, Skills and Knowledge Required:

Job Duties and Responsibilities: Percent of Time Involved:

Supervisory Responsibilities: Yes _____   No _____

Miscellaneous:

_____

Employee Signature   Date

You are strongly encouraged to review your job descriptions to ensure they are gender neutral in language. Job descriptions sometimes take on a life of their own and are not always reviewed from year to year. This, however, is no reason to perpetuate gender-related stereotypes in the way we think about jobs. In addition, be careful that any job skills you list are really necessary for the job. If your description contains requirements that aren't truly needed for the job as it's actually performed, you may be leaving yourself open for significant difficulties in case of a legal challenge.

STARTING THE HIRING PROCESS

Figure 1.9 The Value of Benefits

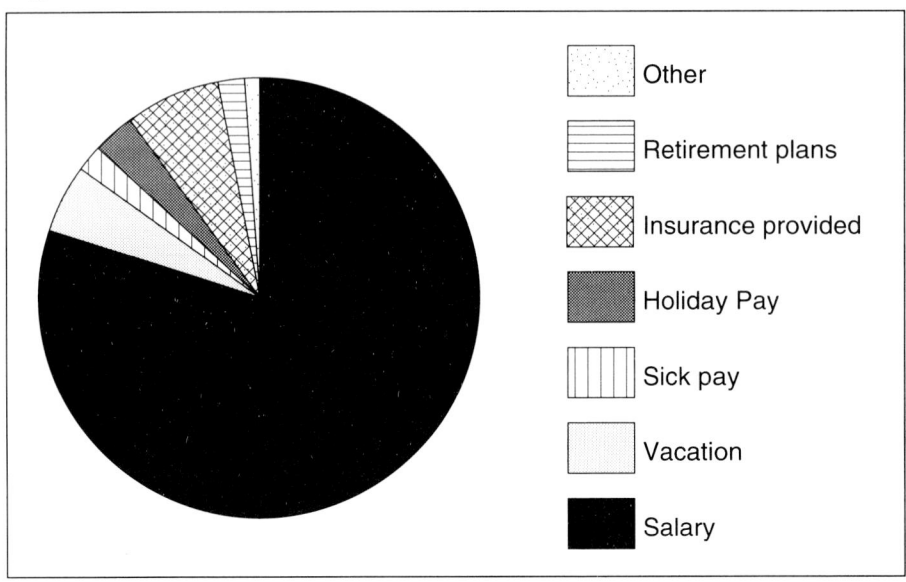

Legend:
- Other
- Retirement plans
- Insurance provided
- Holiday Pay
- Sick pay
- Vacation
- Salary

there are more people than jobs.

If your community has more qualified workers available than jobs for those workers, wages will tend to remain at the lower end of the scale. Your community, however, will have more jobs to offer when the national economy grows stronger.

Informal discussions with your colleagues in the business marketplace at service club meetings, professional groups, or charity board meetings can tell you a lot about the salary environment in your community. Your local chamber of commerce can also provide advice, since it frequently gathers this information to entice new businesses into the area. Another source of information is the office of the local Job Service, the federal office in charge of unemployment compensation.

Activity 1.4

What benefits does your credit union currently offer?

List the benefits a new employee will get when she joins your credit union. Be specific and comprehensive. Once you have exhausted your memory, check with others in the office to see which ones you've missed. Consider all benefits from the new employee's point of view: "What things of tangible value will I get from working here?"

1. _____
2. _____
3. _____
4. _____
5. _____
6. _____
7. _____
8. _____

The Value of a Benefit Package

The impact of benefit value on employees is the subject of much dispute. In the past, employers have generally positioned the benefits of a job as making up an additional 30 percent added to the base salary. When most people are hired for a position, however, the main dollar consideration is the base salary, since this is what determines take-home pay. And the take-home pay is what everyone uses to meet life's expenses. When employers talked about the value of the benefit package, workers of the past tended to pay less attention.

This situation is changing, largely because of the rise in health costs and the financial focus heightened by recent economic conditions. More and more people measure jobs by the value of their benefit packages. With the cost of health insurance steadily climbing, and no short-term relief in sight, your benefit package should play an increasingly important role in determining the attractiveness of employment at your credit union.

Along with the base pay, consider the value of vacation time. In this time of many two-income families, the value of paid vacation has become enhanced. A vacation gives couples time to be together. Their busy work schedules normally don't allow this.

Your insurance supplier should be able to provide you with materials that accent the value of your insurance coverages. The more options you can give your potential employees, the more attractive your benefit package.

For example, the growth in two-worker families means that many families carry duplicate coverage. Why not allow a worker who carries coverage through his or her spouse to take the equivalent value of that coverage in the form of increased salary, or in the form of a coverage not normally offered, such as dental or vision care? There are some restrictions on this practice, but review the possibilities with your insurance supplier.

Today's employees have been hearing for several years that the comfort of their retirement will likely be entirely in their hands. No longer can we count on social security to provide us an era of comfortable twilight years. Regardless of the accuracy of this depiction, people believe it. They're acting on this belief by doing more retirement planning than the generations before.

You can sweeten your salary offer by developing a pension or retirement plan to which the credit union makes a matching contribution up to a certain ceiling. You can offer free financial planning or retirement counseling to your employees through a local financial services firm. Many credit unions offer these services to their members. Why not make them equally available to your own employees? Again, these factors enhance the value of the base salary and make the job increasingly attractive to the quality prospect.

Employee assistance programs provide help to workers or family members facing problems with addictive behaviors of many types. In today's world, this service to employees can help salvage a valued employee who's run up against some personal difficulties. And its mention in your benefits package suggests your caring attitude toward your workers.

Company-provided (for larger credit unions) or company-funded daycare is a hot topic in the nineties, with more and more two-earner families in the workforce. While this benefit isn't cheap, its value in drawing qualified applicants is real. Review the possibilities for your employees. Some larger firms are able to start up their own centers, while other contract with existing area centers for the service.

The same high appeal applies to health club memberships, even if your credit union can only contribute to reduce the basic fee. This type of service-mindedness toward your staff members can, for a reasonable dollar expenditure, build considerable

company loyalty, as well as healthier employees. And it can make working for your credit union more attractive to well-qualified job candidates.

Summary

Making good hiring decisions demands considerable objectivity as well as a commitment to avoiding the most common pitfalls in hiring. An exit interview can provide you with the most direct method for ensuring the accuracy of a job description. This is critical, since all hiring and assessing of employees must legally depend on their job descriptions and the skills outlined there. Every time you hire for a position, you should analyze the job to ensure the description remains accurate and complete. In presenting the job to the applicant, you should be prepared to talk knowledgeably about salary level and the credit union's benefit package.

Chapter Two: Creating a Pool of Applicants

There are several fruitful approaches to obtaining qualified applicants. You should consider them all, depending on the size of your community and the state of the local job market.

Your Existing Resume and Application File

You may have the answer to filling the opening right in your files. Most credit unions receive a regular flow of resumes and applications. Your first step in prospecting for applicants is to review the contents of this file. In fact, if you *don't* look over the material in this file, you may well leave yourself open to charges of discrimination. If your credit union already has knowledge of an applicant whose skills match those needed by the vacant position, you have an *obligation* to consider that person for the job.

Newspaper Advertising

Newspaper advertising has traditionally been the first choice for credit union employee recruiting, and it continues to deliver a strong source of applicants. Such advertising has many benefits:

- It's relatively simple to put together an ad that spells out the qualifications you need.
- Newspaper advertising gar-

Objectives

> **Upon completion of this chapter, you will be able to:**
> 1. **Write recruitment ads and determine the best places for them to run.**
> 2. **Evaluate the use of employment agencies in recruiting new workers.**
> 3. **Examine the pool of current employees as a source of referrals and applicants to fill a vacancy.**

ners wide circulation, and the classified ads are read by almost everyone seeking employment, even those currently employed.
- The cost is generally quite reasonable.
- Through the use of a blind box ("Reply to box number 243."), you can avoid excessive phone calls. Blind box advertising, however, tends to put a damper on responses from employed people, since they may wind up sending a resume to their current employer!
- You should know that some people feel employers who use blind boxes are a little ashamed of their companies.
- The more specific you make your advertising, the more qualified the applicants you will receive. For example, advertise for someone with spreadsheet skills on a DOS-based microcomputer, rather

than for someone with computer skills.

You can gain some expertise in writing ads by studying the classifieds to see how others compose their help wanted ads. Your local newspaper can also give you tips on formatting your ad.

Employment Agencies (including the Federal Job Service)

Employment agencies (or executive recruiting services, as they are called when targeting high-salary employees) can prove a valuable ally in recruiting, especially if your labor marketplace is thin. Some services span the nation, with offices in most siz-

---

Activity 2.1

Create some recruitment ads for your credit union.

Put together three different newspaper ads for your credit union—one advertising for a teller position, one for a bookkeeping position, and one for a new accounts person. Use your knowledge of your credit union's operations to list the important prerequisites needed for these positions. The more words you use, the more expensive the ad. Keep the word count for each ad under sixty. And remember, you want to *attract* candidates, not scare them away. Sample ads are given in appendix A for comparison once you've completed this activity.

Teller Position Ad

_____

_____

_____

_____

_____

_____

Bookkeeping Position Ad

_____

_____

_____

_____

_____

_____

New Accounts Person Ad

_____

_____

_____

_____

_____

_____

_____

able cities. Other employment agencies are small, independent operations. Many employment agencies (especially the larger ones with widespread computer networks) know about people moving into the area. All of these agencies, large and small, can reduce your time in regular hiring by "pre-qualifying" prospects. In other words, you provide the agency with the minimum qualifications you need and it will refer to you only applicants who meet those standards. This method can save you time—you end up interviewing only those applicants who have passed a qualifying screening conducted by the employment agency.

Some agencies specialize in different segments of the labor force. A large community may actually have firms that focus their attention on job applicants in the financial services area. This will be more helpful for those credit unions seeking applicants for other than entry-level positions.

Recruitment and employment agencies also provide you a degree of anonymity. Some managers are concerned with confidentiality in their search for new employees. They don't want people to know their credit union is seeking a new employee. They want to keep employee turnover from the public. Most managers recognize this isn't a very grave concern. Ours is a mobile, dynamic society. Looking for employees can just as easily be a sign of growth as it is of turnover.

The services of an employment agency are not free. You will generally pay a percentage of your new employee's first-year salary to the agency in compensation for its services. The range is between 15 and 25 percent. Only you can judge whether such an expense is worthwhile for your credit union. You should make this decision based on your workload, the labor market in your agency, and the speed with which you have to fill your vacancy.

Some temporary employment agencies can provide bonded employees, whose honesty is insured by a bonding company. In the unlikely instance of embezzlement or theft by one of these temporaries, the bonding company would compensate your credit union for the monetary loss.

The Federal Job Service, administered by the state governments, has offices in most large communities and can also provide a source of applicants for your positions. Job Service screening may not be as thorough as that offered by the private agencies, but you pay no fee. Putting in a little more time in screening may yield you significant savings. Most Job Service offices have a special number for employers to call to place job listings. Check your local Yellow Pages.

Some communities, apart from Job Service, have job placement programs for disadvantaged and minority citizens. Cities and counties will sometimes pay for the training of new workers, who then return to the workforce to become productive, tax-paying members of the community. Contact your local county or municipal government for details on programs in your area.

The Federal Job Service, administered by the state governments, has offices in most large communities and can also provide a source of applicants for your positions.

School Recruiting

Depending on your community and its labor pool, your recruiting efforts will vary. Where the labor market is a tight one, working with area schools can provide an effective pipeline of educated employees. Much will depend on the position for which you are hiring, but local high school counselors are always eager to hear of entry-level openings for new graduates.

In areas with dynamic vocational and business schools, credit unions can find a large and generally well-trained pool of workers for employment in the financial marketplace. Contact with any of these institutions will guide you to the best steps for introducing yourself to applicants. Many schools have well-developed internships or work-study programs to match up businesses with students seeking training in a particular line of work. Such positions sometimes include a partial subsidy of salary during an initial training period. For more information on such programs, talk to the schools in your area.

Referrals, Especially from Employees

Many companies have had considerable success using their current employees as a source of new employee applications. Current staff know the workplace demands of the credit union (and the particular job), as well as the personal qualities of their friends and relatives. This can provide a real shortcut, especially if you are able to establish a formal referral program.

There are downsides to this in-house referral system. Imagine one of your valued employees recommending her best friend for a newly-opened position in your credit union. She's a perfect match, your employee tells you. But once you review the resumes, go through the interviews, and summarize your findings about all the candidates, it's clear your employee's friend isn't your first choice. You can imagine the disappointed response from your employee when the best friend is not chosen for the job.

Referrals from in-house might also lead to the situation of having friends or relatives supervising one another—never a good situation. And it can serve to keep new blood and new ideas from coming into your workplace.

There is a recognized advantage to hiring referrals of employees: there's a better chance of close working relationships developing—a real team spirit, not to mention the increased likelihood of carpooling.

Temporary Agencies

One alternative growing in popularity is to utilize temporary agencies as a source for full-time employees. These temporary agencies are sometimes stand-alone operations, dealing solely in *temps*. Often, however, they're a division of a full-time employment agency.

As you probably know, temporary agencies help many service companies get through trying times. They provide capable people to work without the expenses to the employer of benefits and long-term commitment. The company pays the agency, and the agency forwards to the individual a percentage of the fee, normally about 60 percent.

Hiring temporary workers for full-time employment is not unprincipled. There's nothing dishonest or unethical in this practice, provided you follow the temporary agency's rules regarding the hiring of its workers.

Most agencies recognize that one of the purposes for which workers hire out with these agencies is to secure the contacts which might lead to full-time employment. In general, your contract with the temporary agency obligates you to pay a fee to cover their costs in locating, hiring, and referring this person to you. In effect, you initially agreed to use a worker part-time and then changed your mind. It's only reasonable that the agency be compensated for the permanent loss of the employee. Most agencies will release this temp for compensation of 10–15 percent of the applicant's first-year salary.

For your part, the primary advantage of this approach is that you get to try before you buy. You have the opportunity to put an individual in the precise working conditions under which he would continue to work. You

can try them out there for several months to watch job performance, adaptability to the current work force, work habits, and so on. In fact, you'll probably get to know this person better than you knew the rest of your employees before you hired them.

The Pool of Current Employees as an Option

Many employers have a practice of offering current employees the opportunity to apply for an opening before looking at outside candidates. Internal job postings are a common practice. This posting should include all relevant information about the job, including the salary range. You should encourage employees, by specific mention in the job posting, to contact you for further information about the job. This kind of open-mindedness toward promotions to fill an opening will net positive returns in employee–management relations, as well as in the smooth functioning of the organization. Whatever your policy is in this area, it should be fully spelled out in your employee handbook and other relevant materials.

Listed here are some advantages and disadvantages of filling a position with a current employee.

On the plus side:
- Employees will see they have opportunities for advancement, and morale will rise.
- If you view your training as an investment you make in an employee, promoting a current employee to a higher

position maximizes your training investment. Your training burden will be lighter with existing employees.

- You will be dealing with a known commodity. You're already aware of the applicant's strengths and weaknesses.

On the negative side:

- In general, you're better off in hiring from the largest pool of applicants. If you restrict your search to insiders, you limit your possibilities.
- By hiring an insider, you have created another opening to fill. This can lead to an on-going case of "musical desks," in which one departure can lead to many different job switches. It's jokingly said that one utility-related industry had become so dependent on insider hiring that, when the president retired, a new office apprentice was hired. Everyone in the organization simply moved up one slot.
- Insider hiring tends to reinforce the existing ways of doing things. This has its strengths, but it can also lead to a gradual loss of inventiveness through injection of new ideas.
- Ignoring the outside employee pool may tend to breed a complacent attitude in current employees. They may lose their competitiveness.

- Hiring from within may create potential legal problems related to any affirmative action responsibilities you may have. It may also raise concerns about discrimination.

Of course, bringing in someone from outside can also create friction within a credit union. This can be especially true when the existing staff has worked together for some time, and the person who left was well-liked. Many people like to hire from inside because they feel their credit union is unique and that it will take an outsider a long time to understand just how the operation works. People who look at companies (including credit unions) from the outside understand that truly unique companies are exceedingly rare.

Summary

Getting the best people for your credit union means you have to actively recruit applicants. The more people you evaluate, the more likely you will find what you need. Newspaper advertising is a time-honored technique for drawing applicants. Employment agencies and temporary agencies can also provide candidates. Your current staff can prove helpful, both through their referrals of friends, and through their own in-house applications to fill staff vacancies.

Chapter Three: Reading a Resume

A resume summarizes a person's basic identifying information and qualifications for a job. A complete resume includes the applicant's name and address, educational history, employment history, and significant specialized experience. It should also provide, or offer to provide upon request, people you can call for further information on the applicant.

Resumes go through as many fashion changes as clothing styles. Chronological resumes, skill resumes, topical resumes, and others cross management desks every day. Understanding just what these resumes actually represent has become more and more difficult.

A straightforward tip: Unless you select a staff person from your human resources department, don't have someone go through the resumes to conduct a first sort before you get to them yourself. As you'll see, judging people from resumes and job applications is difficult enough work. It demands your full attention, unless you're prepared to take the chance of passing up a truly special person—one that might not be recognized in a one-minute screening job.

There's a second reason why you should do this screening yourself: respect for the applicants. They've gone to the trouble of spotting your advertisement, making a copy of their resume, writing you a cover letter, and

Objectives

> **Upon completion of this chapter, you will be able to:**
>
> 1. **Evaluate all parts of a resume, and especially work history, for the requirements of a particular job opening.**
>
> 2. **Contact references and obtain job-related information on an applicant.**
>
> 3. **Create an evaluation grid on which to rate all job applicants objectively.**

A resume summarizes a person's basic identifying information and qualifications for a job. A complete resume includes the applicant's name and address, educational history, employment history, and significant specialized experience.

buying a stamp. They deserve your best attention.

Sometimes you simply can't do this screening. Perhaps the pool of applicants is too large. Or you are in the midst of annual budgeting. If you can't do this job, ask a trusted subordinate to handle the initial screening. You still have the responsibility to work through enough resumes to make your staff member knowledgeable about the hiring and screening process. Review a number of applications closely, making sure she understands the details of the job description and exactly why you're accepting or rejecting each applicant. Only when you're confident your subordinate understands the standards by which you would judge the applicants can you relinquish the screening task.

Looking Over and Through the Resume

Resumes aren't designed to deliver information; they're not designed to get jobs, they are designed to get interviews. You're getting one person's best efforts to make herself seem employable. Figures 3.1 and 3.2 include sample resumes that show the type of information usually provided by job applicants. The applicant's resume is only a starting point. You should have all applicants provide a resume and fill out your standard credit union job application. They can either stop by the credit union to pick up an application, or you can mail one to everyone who sends in a resume. Application forms can be important because some resumes fail to give written permission to call references, while others fail to name references at all. A good application, like the one shown in figure 3.6, provides you with permission from applicants to contact references. This permission, in writing, could prove valuable should your hiring practices ever be questioned due to an unfavorable reference. A good job application, coupled with your skills as an interviewer, will tell you what you want to know to make your decision on which applicants to interview.

In the same fashion that

you're reading this manual to learn how to be a better interviewer and hirer, so your potential applicants are reading their job-hunting and resume-writing books to learn how to make the very best impression on you. The battle for good jobs is escalating, with heavy weaponry on both sides: hirers and would-be hirees. You need to read between the lines of any resume you receive.

In general, you will find that the experience and education sections of most resumes tend to be in inverse proportion. With less education, more work experience information is usually listed; the more education, the less work experience. This is only natural. The more years spent in school, the less time available for on-the-job experience.

As we all know, you should look for gaps in employment or educational records. Your job isn't to uncover any dark secrets, but you should satisfy yourself with what was happening during that time. Was the person working in a job that would give him a bad reference? Was the person unemployed? Are there gaps relevant to a hiring decision?

Sometimes a resume is more revealing than it intends to be. If spelling and typing are important qualifications for a position, how might you react to receiving a resume filled with spelling errors and poorly-corrected typing errors?

Keep yourself open-minded. If you approach the job of hiring someone as simply taking the path of least risk and resistance, you're liable to wind up with

Figure 3.1 A Sample Resume

JANE SMITH
4095 West Broadway
Cumberland, MD 21502
Home: (301)828-7654
Office: (301)828-3952

WORK EXPERIENCE:

1985–Present   CHESSIE FEDERAL CREDIT UNION   Cumberland, MD
Operations Analyst

Responsible for: developing proposals to top management for operational reviews; orga-
nizing and managing the task forces to conduct the reviews; documenting and presenting
recommendations to top management; coordinating this credit union's efforts with similar
initiatives in the Federal Reserve System. Major accomplishments include:
- Initiated, systematized, and managed a review of credit union examinations and
  applications processing activities, resulting in annual savings of $1,500,000.
- Developed long-range plan, necessary capital, and operating budgets for the 185-
  person International Services Department; analyzed costs of foreign exchange and
  investment transactions.

1983–1985   UNITED NATIONS DEVELOPMENT PROGRAM   New York, NY
Planning Officer
Responsible for program planning, resource allocation, and evaluation of a $100 million
program of technical and capital assistance to developing countries in the area of popula-
tion control and economic development. Major accomplishments include:
- Organized and supervised a ten-month, fifteen-person study of the world contracep-
  tive market, sponsored jointly by UNDP and the Ford Foundation.
- Developed a model-based forecasting system for program planning,
  management, and control.
- Developed population control projects for countries in East Africa and the Middle
  East.

EDUCATION:

1987   NEW YORK UNIVERSITY, Graduate School of Business
Ph.D., International Banking

1983   MASSACHUSETTS INSTITUTE OF TECHNOLOGY
M.S., Management

1969   RUTGERS UNIVERSITY
B.S., Physics

Figure 3.2 An Additional Sample Resume

DAVID SUMMERS
5705 Deer Run Road
Columbia, SC 97532
(803)781-3851

MANAGEMENT:

- Hired telephone consultant engineers, training them in technical and interpersonal communications.
- Successfully expanded this group from three to fifteen.
- Developed career path strategy and created charts with management for levels ranging from telephone consultant to project engineers.

TRAINING:

- Trained over 150 people, over ten months, including senior executives, critical care area managers, salesmen, and field engineers.
- Established task analysis and course objectives for these trainees.
- Applied critical judgment and professional competence in instructing over 85 field personnel in various locations.

ADMINISTRATION:

- Handled inventory of technical education department.
- Organized information for budget and delivered to management.
- Supervised small group responsible for maintaining logistics for telephone central operations.
- Developed telephone call sheet formats that were later computerized, resulting in failure analysis reports now used nationwide.

TECHNICAL:

- Responsible for instruction on mini and micro computer-controlled biomedical instrumentation.
- Developed troubleshooting procedures and charts on assigned instrumentation for customer and field service manuals.
- Served as national technical backup to service engineers on existing and developmental instrumentation.
- Performed the operational maintenance, troubleshooting, repair, retrofit, and updating of in-house production and customer education instrumentation.
- Served as quality control inspector for repair group under my supervision.

1982–Present	TECHNICAL PRODUCTS CORPORATION Technical Instructor	Columbia, SC

EDUCATION:

Current	WESTCHESTER COMMUNITY COLLEGE–Electrical Engineering
1982	Technical Certificate
1979	Electronics Certificate

---

mediocre employees and potential legal problems. If you see the person has spent a long time at each of his or her previous jobs, don't be too quick to view that as positive. Depending on the positions held, and the position you want to fill, those long stints may evidence a lack of ambition. What did the person make of those long stretches of employment? Only your incisive questions in the interview can tell you this.

Be on guard for vagueness. The more qualifications a candidate has, the less need for smoke and mirrors. Resumes, by their very nature, bring out a bit of puffery; but if you have reviewed a resume and still can't figure out what a person did in his or her last two jobs, be prepared to ask a few questions.

Occasionally, you will receive a resume that includes several attached letters of recommendation. These should be given some consideration. Such letters show that someone is willing to put his or her personal stamp of approval on the applicant. To validate the letter for a candidate you're considering seriously, you can simply place a quick call to the writer of the letter to fill in a blank or two—how long he has known the applicant, for example. In some cases, you shouldn't be surprised to find that the writer of the recommending letter has very little actual knowledge of your applicant.

How to Handle References

Before hiring a person for a supervisory position, you should call at least two people from the person's past, either references listed on the resume or provided separately by the applicant, or previous supervisors or managers. While getting an honest reference on an applicant over the phone is not as simple as it used to be, a phone call and inquisitive mind can yield information you can use when making your decision. Form your own opinion from an interview before calling references. This way, references will not influence your initial responses to the candidate.

When you do make you reference calls, make sure you speak with someone who's actually supervised your applicant.

Previous employers may be reluctant to say too much over the phone for fear of legal action from former employees. It's happened. If you talk with the employer frankly, explaining that you're just looking for a general evaluation of your candidate, you can learn a lot from a brief conversation.

If you get a negative response from the most recent job position, don't automatically conclude that your candidate is a poor one. Some relationships in the business world simply are not as smooth as others. Call the employer before that one, assuming the last position didn't last more than a few years. If you find that the two most recent employers start to paint a pattern of undesirability, you should consider switching your attention to another candidate.

When you make your reference calls, make sure you speak with someone who's actually supervised your applicant. Your job application should require the listing of the actual supervisor. You don't want to waste your time talking with someone who's simply handled your applicant's personnel file. If the supervisor listed on the application has left or is unavailable, ask if there's another person there familiar with your applicant's work habits. If necessary, you might even talk with a co-worker to get some idea of how well your applicant did while on the job. Co-worker references deserve some caution, since a reference check like this will generally yield only positive information. Most companies will not allow co-workers to give evaluations; generally they will refer all requests for such evaluations to the personnel department.

If judging the merit of candidates presents a difficult task, judging the value of a reference can be even more challenging. After all, you are trying to make a judgment on another individual's opinion of your applicant. Generally, you're not going to know anything about the person who gives the reference other than position, company, and phone number. It's good practice to use the reference information only as one part of your overall decision-making process. If you

learn something bad about your candidate from a reference, try to verify it through another source. You don't want to pass up a good applicant just because you fell for a vengeful lie told by a former supervisor. It's happened.

On the other hand, if you talk to a reference who praises your candidate to the skies, be a little skeptical, especially if you're talking to the most recent employer. Perhaps the employer simply wants the person to leave the company; or he may want him employed elsewhere as soon as possible. Remember, in many cases, as soon as an ex-employee gets a job, the deductions from the previous employer's unemployment compensation account discontinues. That's a solid financial incentive for a former employer to spin a tale of competence for an inept ex-employee.

When talking to the references, don't forget to ask some obvious questions: Did the candidate show up for work on time? Were there unexplained absences? Work from the simple to the more complex issues.

Make your approach to the reference nonthreatening. After all, the reference is doing you a favor in donating time to help with your job search. So you want to assure her that you're not expecting a lengthy interview or a comprehensive search of past employee files. In other words, don't make your request for a reference check seem like a task. Instead, make it two business colleagues talking to one another about an item of mutual interest. Make the interview as painless as possible.

Figures 3.3 and 3.4 offer two different samples of forms you can use while on the phone with a reference. These give you insight into the types of questions asked to determine applicant information. They can also be mailed to the reference for completion and return. An authorization for information release may be necessary if you decide to use this mail method. Many references will not release information without authorization from the individual concerned. Information release areas are sometimes included in the employment application form. When sending these forms in the mail, include a self-addressed, stamped envelope for their return. Use the same reference checking form for all applicants pursuing a particular job. A standard form helps to ensure all candidates receive fair and equal treatment. Remember to keep all questions job related and to record the name of the person providing the information. If the reference source will not provide performance related information, be sure to note your attempt to obtain the information on the form.

Sometimes credit union managers and senior executives forget they're hiring people to work in close contact with other people's money. Security should never be far from your mind in all hiring. Don't let your innocence or enthusiasm for a candidate lull you into hiring without checking references. Most crime against financial institutions comes from inside, and the planting of employees by con artists inside a financial institution to take part in a quick-hit scheme is not unheard of.

Let's assume, for the moment, that you hire a candidate without checking on the references listed on the resume. And let's assume that person then proceeds to embezzle, or just plain steal, money from your credit union. Have you been negligent in hiring that person? The point here is that you have a fiduciary responsibility to check on a serious candidate's references before making that candidate an employee at your financial institution. Even if your insurance company protects you, you may need to respond to your members questions about the soundness of your hiring practices should a new employee embezzle from your credit union.

The hiring experts agree on the absolute need to check references. Research indicates that perhaps one-third of all applicants falsify some statements on their applications, and all will put a happy face on the facts of their past employment. Think of your own past jobs. Would you and your past employers tell the same tale of any past disagreements? If you don't check references, you're simply taking the lazy way out. You are taking the applicant's word on the content of past job history.

In fact, some people argue that if you don't check references, the dishonest applicant will know it. And he will come to some negative conclusions about your thoroughness. If you let an applicant get by with a lie on an application, you may be setting yourself and your credit union

Figure 3.3 Reference Checking Info Form

Reference Checking Information

Date _____

Name of Applicant _____

Former Supervisor _____

_____

Company Where Worked   City & State   Telephone Number

1. _____ has applied for employment with our company and we would like to verify some information given us. What were the dates of employment with your company? _____
    _____

2. What was the nature of his work? _____
    _____

3. What did you think of his performance? _____
    _____
    _____

4. Was close supervision required? _____

5. How well did he get along with other people? _____
    _____

6. Did he have good attendance? _____

7. Why did he leave? _____
    _____

8. Would you reemploy _____? Yes ____ No ____ If no, why? _____
    _____

9. What are his outstanding points? _____
    _____
    _____

10. What are his weak points? _____
    _____
    _____

11. How would you rank quality of work?   Above Average   Average   Unsatisfactory
    (circle one)

12. How would you rank quantity of work?   Above Average   Average   Unsatisfactory
    (circle one)

                                                Signed _____
                                                (Individual making reference check)

Comments: _____
_____
_____
_____
_____

Figure 3.4 Confidential Reference Information Form

Confidential Reference Information

Name of Applicant: _____

Social Security Number: _____

Period Employed: _____

Nature of Work: _____

_____

_____

Reason for Leaving Your Employ: _____

_____

Would You Rehire? _____ If No, Why Not? _____

_____

_____

	Excellent	Satisfactory	Unsatisfactory
Quality of Work	_____	_____	_____
Quantity of Work	_____	_____	_____
Planning/Organizing Ability	_____	_____	_____
Working With Other People	_____	_____	_____
Dependability	_____	_____	_____
Initiative	_____	_____	_____
_____	_____	_____	_____
_____	_____	_____	_____

Additional Remarks: _____

_____

_____

_____

_____

_____

Signed: _____

Signature/Date

---

up for some real trouble. Play it safe. Make the calls and verify the work habits of your top candidates and the accuracy of their application materials.

Checking a current employer reference can be tricky. Most applicants don't want their current employer to know they are looking for another job. Yet, if you hire without talking to that employer, you're omitting the most recent evidence in the work skills of your applicant.

One way used to get around this difficulty is to make a firm offer of employment, but make it contingent upon speaking with the current employer. In effect, you're telling the applicant you will only talk to the current boss if the job offer you're making is a firm one pending reference

check. Of course, if that boss reveals something unacceptable, the job offer can be withdrawn.

Depending on the importance of the position you're filling (and your own time schedule), checking a reference with a brief personal meeting represents the strongest approach to verifying past job experience. In a smaller town or city, this may be a very reasonable alternative to a phone call. You will learn things through personal contact that are never learned over the phone.

If your applicant has been bonded while working at another credit union, you can check with CUNA Mutual to verify performance.

The Job Application

A good job application provides you with the basic background on an applicant, minus the embellishment provided by the resume. An application should include

- Name, address, and contact information
- Employment history
- Specific skills and knowledge
- Job goals
- Education

Once you receive resumes in the mail, you should conduct a brief review of each and decide which candidates merit your further attention.

At this stage of the hiring process, all applicants should have stopped by the credit union to pick up a formal job application. Send the applicants a letter telling them you have received their resumes and would like

Figure 3.5 Phone Reference Checklist

Use this list to outline the questions you want to ask a reference during a phone call.

- Applicant's name
- Name and company of reference
- Reference phone
- Notes on attempts made to reach reference
- Dates of applicant employment
- Job title and type of work applicant actually performed
- Reference's precise work relationship with applicant
- Approximate ending salary level
- Applicant's promotions or disciplinary actions
- Was applicant on time and present on a regular basis?
- Level of satisfaction with applicant's performance
- Why did applicant leave your company?
- Would you rehire?
- Other comments
- Interviewer name and date

Note: *A cautious previous employer would be prudent **not** to answer several of these questions. Be prepared to be hear the response "I'd rather not comment on that."*

Figure 3.6 A Sample Job Application

Credit Union National Association, Inc.

For use by: CUNA, Inc. • CUNA Service Group, Inc. • CUNA Mortgage • World Council of Credit Unions, Inc.
5710 Mineral Point Rd., Box 431, Madison, WI 53701-0431 (608) 231-4801

U.S. Central Credit Union • 7300 College Blvd., Suite 600, Overland Park, KS 66210 (913) 661-3800
CUNA Washington • 805 15th Street NW, Suite 300, Washington, DC 20005-2207 (202) 682-4200

Date _____

We request the following information to help us make the best possible placement. You should complete all portions of this application that pertain to you. We appreciate the time you spend in completing this form.

If offered employment and accepted, you are required by law to show proof of eligibility to work in the USA.

If offered employment and accepted, you are required by law to show you are 18 years of age or over.

Name _____ Former Name _____
        LAST   FIRST   MI

Home Telephone No. _____ / _____ Alternate Telephone No. _____ / _____

Address _____
              STREET   CITY   STATE   ZIP CODE

Do you have any relatives in our employment?   ☐ Yes   ☐ No   If so, please list. _____

Have you ever filed an application with us before?   ☐ Yes   ☐ No   If Yes, give date. _____

Have you ever been employed with us before?   ☐ Yes   ☐ No   If yes, give date. _____

Referred to this company by: _____

Position for which you are applying _____ Salary Desired _____

Employment Preference: ☐ Full time   ☐ Part time   Date available _____

                         ☐ Summer   ☐ Temporary   Dates/Hours available _____

Education — Military Training

NAME	ADDRESS	MAJOR COURSE/ SUBJECT	CIRCLE LAST YEAR COMPLETED				DID YOU GRADUATE?	DEGREE
High School			1	2	3	4	☐ Yes ☐ No	
Business/Trade School			1	2	3	4	☐ Yes ☐ No	
College			1	2	3	4	☐ Yes ☐ No	
Graduate Studies			1	2	3	4	☐ Yes ☐ No	
Other (specify)			1	2	3	4	☐ Yes ☐ No	

Are you currently pursuing further studies? ☐ Yes   ☐ No

If so, what courses and when? _____

Figure 3.6 A Sample Job Application–*continued*   *page 2*

Have you been convicted of a criminal offense within the last 7 years?

· ☐ Yes   ☐ No   If yes, please explain.

_____

_____

· A CONVICTION WILL NOT NECESSARILY BE A BAR TO EMPLOYMENT AND WILL BE CONSIDERED ONLY AS IT RELATES TO POSITION APPLIED FOR.

Machine Operation: Check which machines you can operate

☐ Typewriter _____ wpm   ☐ Adding machine/calculator

☐ Shorthand _____ wpm   ☐ Switchboard

☐ Data Entry Terminal _____ kph   ☐ Dictaphone

☐ Personal computer   ☐ Other (specify) _____

☐ Hardware/Software

Can you travel if job requires it: ☐ Yes   ☐ No

Indicate what foreign languages you speak, read, and/or write.

	FLUENTLY	GOOD	FAIR
SPEAK			
READ			
WRITE			

References:

Please list names, addresses and phone numbers of two work references.

Phone no. _____ / _____   Phone no. _____ / _____

Figure 3.6 A Sample Job Application–*continued*   *page 3*

Applicant Data Record

Credit Union National Association, Inc.

Human Resource Department (Madison)	Human Resource Department (Overland Pk)	CUNA Washington
5710 Mineral Point Road, Box 431	7300 College Blvd., Suite 600	805 15th Street NW Suite 300
Madison, WI 53701-0431	Overland, KS 66210 • 913-661-3800	Washington, DC 20005-2207
608-231-4801		(202) 682-4200

All qualified applicants will receive consideration for employment without regard to sex, race, color, national origin or ancestry, age, handicap, marital status, source of income, class, physical characteristics, sexual orientation, less than honorable discharge, or political beliefs. No information on this application will be used for the purpose of such discrimination.

We comply with government regulations and affirmative action responsibilities. Solely to help us comply with government record keeping, reporting and other legal requirements, please fill out the Applicant Data Record. This data is for analysis and affirmative action purposes only, and submission of this information is voluntary. Government agencies require periodic reports on the sex, ethnicity, handicapped and veteran status of applicants. This data will be kept in a Confidential File separate from the Application for Employment. We appreciate your cooperation.

Date _____

Position Applied For _____

Name _____ Phone (____) _____
      LAST   FIRST   MIDDLE   AREA CODE

Address _____
      NUMBER   STREET   CITY   STATE   ZIP

Affirmative Action Survey

Check one:

☐ Male   ☐ Female

Check one of the following:

☐ Race/Ethnic Group: ☐ White ☐ Black ☐ Hispanic

          ☐ American Indian/Alaskan Native   Asian/Pacific Island

Check if any of the following are applicable:

☐ Vietnam Era Veteran   ☐ Disabled Veteran   ☐ Handicapped Individual*

Please use the back of this sheet to explain any special accommodations that you may require in order to do the job for which you are applying.

Figure 3.6 A Sample Job Application–*continued*   *page 4*

Employment history: *

Please list below present and past employment, to include military service, **beginning with the most recent.** Please complete **all** items and be specific.

*If you have a resume, attach it to the application. Please complete information on the application that is not supplied on the resume.

1 COMPANY | **ADDRESS** | **TELEPHONE**

DATES EMPLOYED
FROM: TO: | **SALARY**
STARTING: LEAVING: | **NAME OF SUPERVISOR**

YOUR TITLE | **YOUR DUTIES**

REASON FOR LEAVING

2 COMPANY | **ADDRESS** | **TELEPHONE**

DATES EMPLOYED
FROM: TO: | **SALARY**
STARTING: LEAVING: | **NAME OF SUPERVISOR**

YOUR TITLE | **YOUR DUTIES**

REASON FOR LEAVING

3 COMPANY | **ADDRESS** | **TELEPHONE**

DATES EMPLOYED
FROM: TO: | **SALARY**
STARTING: LEAVING: | **NAME OF SUPERVISOR**

YOUR TITLE | **YOUR DUTIES**

REASON FOR LEAVING

4 COMPANY | **ADDRESS** | **TELEPHONE**

DATES EMPLOYED
FROM: TO: | **SALARY**
STARTING: LEAVING: | **NAME OF SUPERVISOR**

YOUR TITLE | **YOUR DUTIES**

REASON FOR LEAVING

May we contact the above employers for reference checking purposes? _____

Please identify by number any employer you do **not** wish us to contact? _____

Figure 3.6 A Sample Job Application–*continued*   *page 5*

ADDITIONAL COMMENTS—OPTIONAL: Use the space below to describe your interest in the companies and the skills and experience that you feel qualify you for a position with us. You may wish to include participation in, professional societies and/or, special training or skills. Do not list organizations which reveal race, creed, color, national origin, age or sex.

LAST NAME

FIRST

_____

_____

_____

_____

_____

_____

_____

_____

_____

_____

_____

—PLEASE READ CAREFULLY BEFORE SIGNING—

MIDDLE INITIAL

All qualified applicants will receive consideration for employment without regard to sex, race, color, national origin or ancestry, age, handicap, marital status, source of income, class, physical characteristics, sexual orientation, or political beliefs, etc. as prohibited by Federal or State Laws. No information on this application will be used for the purpose of discrimination.

I understand that receipt of this application by CUNA Inc. does not guarantee a job interview or offer of employment.

POSITION

I voluntarily grant CUNA Inc. the right to investigate and verify the information and statements I have provided in this application.

I understand that the employment that may be offered is not guaranteed for any particular length of time and that either CUNA Inc. or I remain free to terminate the relationship at any time.

I certify that the statements I have made on this application are true. I understand that falsification of any statements made by me on this application is grounds for disqualification from further consideration or for immediate dismissal from employment.

APPLICANT'S SIGNATURE: _____   DATE SIGNED: _____

EEOC

FOR HR USE ONLY

LOG

OFFER MADE?   BY: DATE: ACCEPTED?

SALARY: STARTING DATE: DEPARTMENT:

JOB TITLE: SUPERVISOR: HOURS:

them to fill out the job application and return it within three or four working days.

Figure 3.6 shows a sample job application which organized information in a clear and complete fashion. This application was updated in January 1991 to comply with the Americans with Disabilities Act. You may use this application as a model for creating your own or visit an office supply store to review and select from the many styles available. Figure 3.7 is a special application to be used by current employees applying for a another position in your institution. This process is sometimes called an internal bid.

Evaluating Employment History

There is no escaping the fact that the recent past is the best indicator of near-future performance. The most important part of a resume or job application is the employment history. Some individuals do very well in school, but have a difficult time with the discipline of the work environment.

What should you look for in the employment history portion of the resume/application?

- Job duration. Was the applicant in previous jobs long enough to justify employer time, cost, and energy in hiring and bringing the applicant to full performance level? If the work history shows frequent changes, do the changes show an upward progression?
- Types of skills used. Do the jobs listed on the application show that the person has experience with the types of skills you need for your job? If you're looking for a teller, for example, does the applicant's job history show significant contact with people and some facility in dealing with money?
- Job title and level of responsibility. Has the applicant shown the ability to handle responsibility? Was there any supervisory skill needed in previous jobs?
- Clarity of previous job duties. Everyone has a tendency to inflate their work history. If it's not easily inflatable, then many people will tend to be vague about exactly what it is they did. If past jobs look a little murky on the application, probe for specifics during the interview.
- Did the person work as part of a team, or independently? Generally, you're looking for a team player, someone who can work closely with all the departments in your credit union. If the person held jobs which fostered a loose approach to work (like outside sales person, route person, or independent contractor), you may need to bring this issue up in the interview.
- Are recent employers listed as references?
- Are there any gaps? Again, this may not present a problem, but a lengthy gap between jobs should lead you to raise the question in the interview.

Figure 3.7 A Sample Internal Job Application   *front*

INTERNAL APPLICATION

Name _____   Date _____

Position Applying For _____   Telephone Ext. _____

The information you provide on this application will determine your eligibility for the position for which you are applying. It is extremely important that you include all job-related information requested. To help us more accurately evaluate your qualifications, please answer the following statements as they pertain to this particular position. Cite specific examples from your past education and work experience, (i.e., course work, job duties, special projects).

---

1. Training or education **that meets the qualifications** for the posted job.

2. Experience or skills **that meets the qualifications** for the posted job.

3. Other background that qualifies you for the posted job.

4. Why are you interested in the posted job?

HRM-202 (Revised 1/24/91)

Figure 3.7 A Sample Internal Job Application–*continued*   *back*

CURRENT POSITION

Company _____ Department _____

Position Title _____ Supervisor _____

Start Date _____

Duties/Responsibilities:

PREVIOUS EXPERIENCE

(Should include internal departments and/or all previous employers in chronological order.)

Employer/Dept. _____ Supervisor _____

Position Title _____ From _____ To _____

Reason for leaving _____

Duties/Responsibilities:

Employer/Dept. _____ Supervisor _____

Position Title _____ From _____ To _____

Reason for leaving _____

Duties/Responsibilities:

Employer/Dept. _____ Supervisor _____

Position Title _____ From _____ To _____

Reason for leaving _____

Duties/Responsibilities:

USE ADDITIONAL SHEETS IF NECESSARY

Evaluating Educational History

A phone call can verify the college education of job applicants. If your job description for the position doesn't mandate a college degree, don't bother to check on the degree of any college-educated applicants. Don't check on high school graduation, but do call to verify associate degrees or certifications.

In times when the job market is tight, more misstatements of fact, especially of educational records, appear on resumes. A five-minute call to the school can establish the accuracy of any listed degrees.

It will be worth your time to evaluate just what education means in the context of your job opening. Some jobs (such as attorneys, accountants, and doctors) mandate specific educational levels. For most other jobs, the relationship between education and suitability for a particular job is much less clear. Perhaps we should look on a person's school record as an indication of how hard the person is willing to work; in other words, a measure of motivation. It's the opinion of many personnel professionals that education is less important in predicting future job success than a person's attitude and proven skills.

The best way to approach the issue of educational requirements for a position is to require a certain educational level or degree of related experience only if really necessary for the job, or as an alternative to some work experience. You may state you

> In times when the job market is tight, more misstatements of fact, especially of educational records, appear on resumes.

prefer both the education and the experience, but you can't prefer the education just for its own sake. Some jobs, but not as many as we'd like to think, need both a certain educational level and significant experience. Unnecessary educational requirements may discriminate against protected minority groups that may have solid alternative work experience.

Asking an open-ended question about why someone majored in a particular subject, or switched between several majors, can lead you to some insights on the individual's personality.

Pursue any indication of student leadership or major involvement in extracurricular activities. Most people in school don't get heavily involved in any activities except for sports. Why was your applicant involved? Might she exhibit that "above and beyond the call of duty" attitude as an employee?

Creating an Evaluation Grid

Another technique used by experienced hirers—and one that will keep you on the right side of any lawsuits resulting from your hiring practices—is the evaluation grid. There are many different types. Some allow you to evaluate several people on a single sheet, others use one sheet per applicant. We've included several versions in figures 3.8, 3.9, and 3.10.

READING A RESUME

The evaluation grid in figure 3.8 allows you to list the names of each of your candidates on the left side of your sheet and the areas of evaluation across the top of the sheet. Evaluate each candidate in each category on a predetermined scale, from lowest to highest. The greater the number of points, the more highly-rated the candidate.

Categories might include education, relevant skills, work experience, language skills, organization skills, financial institution experience, and so on. When using such a grid, you need to decide the weight you give to each category.

Are they all of equal importance? Are some more important than others? If two or more candidates have the same point total, how will you decide between or among them? You can't totally eliminate subjective factors in your decision, but you *can* create a clear, rational decision-making process with fair standards.

The evaluation grid shown in figure 3.9 uses the same rating system but allows you to rate candidates on their responses to specific questions which you predetermine.

Beware of the *halo effect*. If one characteristic impresses

Figure 3.8 Individual Evaluation Grid by Qualifications

Position Selection Sheet	Required Qualifications										Preferred Qualifications					
Candidate																

Date _____ Position_____

Reviewed by _____

you, don't assume the candidate is equally impressive in all areas. Look at each item on its own merit. Imagine, for a moment, that you had a candidate who happened to have competed in the Olympics. This is pretty great stuff. And it would be easy for you to get caught up in the excitement and to ignore the candidate's other qualities. Olympic-level competition certainly tells you about a candidate's energy and perseverance. Don't focus on that glamour fact and forget to review education, job history, and all those other personal factors that make up the whole person. Unless pole vaulting skill is a major component of the position, stay focused on the essential hiring elements. Don't let a single, high-visible positive create a halo that heightens your rating of other characteristics.

Figure 3.9 Evaluation Grid based on Questions

Candidates

Questions

Questions										
1.										
2.										
3.										
4.										
5.										
6.										

Figure 3.10 Candidate Evaluation Form

HR FORM #__
9/91

CANDIDATE EVALUATION

Position _____

Applicant _____ Interview Date _____

MAJOR DUTIES & JOB RESPONSIBILITIES	APPLICANT'S EDUCATION AND EXPERIENCE	RATING
Misc Other:		

_____ Availability for: 2nd Interview _____ Start Date: _____

_____ Best Time to Contact: _____

_____ Bonding   _____ Benefits   _____ References   _____ Salary

_____   _____
Interviewer   Date

Figure 3.11 Interview Evaluation Form

HR FORM #__
9/91

INTERVIEW EVALUATION

Applicant
_____

Position Applied for _____

Education:	Above Require	Meets Require	Below Require	None/ Marginal
_____	____	____	____	____
_____	____	____	____	____

Experience:

_____	____	____	____	____
_____	____	____	____	____
_____	____	____	____	____

Duties/Responsibilities

_____	____	____	____	____
_____	____	____	____	____
_____	____	____	____	____
_____	____	____	____	____

Skills/Knowledge

_____	____	____	____	____
_____	____	____	____	____

Other Criteria

_____	____	____	____	____
_____	____	____	____	____

Available to Start: _____   Salary: _____

Figure 3.11 Interview Evaluation Form–*continued*   *page 2*

Job Knowledge & Strengths: _____

_____

_____

_____

_____

_____

_____

_____

_____

_____

Job Knowledge - Areas Not As Strong: _____

_____

_____

_____

_____

_____

_____

_____

Overall Rating: Match the qualifications of the applicant against the requirements of the job position for which applicant is being considered. Circle your overall rating of this applicant.

Excellent   Above Average   Average   Below Average   Poor

Reviewed:

____ Application   ____ Resume   ____ References

____ Benefits Sum   ____ Job Desc   ____ CU Philos/History

Best time to contact: _____

Interviewer: _____ **Date:** _____

Figure 3.12 Additional Interview Evaluation Form

INTERVIEW EVALUATION

Name of Applicant _____

Position Applied For _____

Date & Time of Interview _____Conf Room_____

Interviewed By _____

****

I. QUALIFICATIONS:

A.   Experience/Education

1.   How much experience in work similar to that for which the applicant is applying?

_____None	_____Three to five years
_____Less than one year	_____Five to ten years
_____One to three years	_____More than 10 years

2.   How related is the applicant's experience to the position applying for?

_____Unrelated
_____Performs similar work 25% of the time
_____Performs similar work 50% of the time
_____Performs similar work 75% of the time
_____Experience is almost identical

3.   Degree and/or equivalent work experience.

_____Less than high school	_____Some graduate work
_____High school graduate	_____Masters in _____
_____Less than college degree	_____Graduate work
_____College degree in _____	_____Ph.D in _____

4.   Does the applicant have enough of the right kind of experience and education to do the job?

_____Yes   _____Possibly   _____No

Figure 3.12 Additional Interview Evaluation Form–*continued*   *page 2*

B.   **Skills:**

1.   Of all skills required for this position, ie. keyboard, personal computer, verbal/written communication, etc, does the employee possess these skills?

List Required Skills

_____	_____Yes	_____No
_____	_____Yes	_____No
_____	_____Yes	_____No
_____	_____Yes	_____No
_____	_____Yes	_____No
_____	_____Yes	_____No
_____	_____Yes	_____No
_____	_____Yes	_____No

Please explain;_____

_____

_____

2.   Of all skills preferred for this position, does the employee possess these skills?

List Preferred Skills

_____	_____Yes	_____No
_____	_____Yes	_____No
_____	_____Yes	_____No
_____	_____Yes	_____No
_____	_____Yes	_____No

Please explain;_____

_____

_____

_____

Figure 3.12 Additional Interview Evaluation Form–*continued*   *page 3*

II. JOB FIT

A. Applicants Objectives

1. Are the applicant's goals compatible with the opportunities offered by this position?

_____Yes   _____No   _____Possibly

2. Why is the applicant seeking this position?

_____Type of work: Explain_____
_____Higher salary, more benefits
_____Promotional Opportunities
_____Dissatisfaction with present position
_____Other; explain_____

_____

B. Work Environment

1. Will the work environment permit the applicant to perform the job effectively?

_____Yes   _____No

Please Explain;_____

_____
_____

2. **Evaluation**

A. Considering factors I & II do you recommend this applicant for this position?

_____Yes   _____Possibly   _____No

If yes, would you like Human Resources to extend an offer at this time?

_____Yes   _____No

Comments:_____
_____
_____
_____

Signature & Date _____

READING A RESUME

Activity 3.1
Create Your Own Interview Grid

Many interviewers create a grid to use during interviews with each candidate for the same job. It helps them compare candidates after the interviews are completed by assigning specific numbers to candidates for the questions asked during the interview. Consider you are interviewing for a new teller position. Using the form provided in figure 3.9, create a list of six questions which you will ask all applicants. Remember to keep your questions strictly job-related.

Sample answers can be found in appendix A at the back of this book.

Summary

A resume and application can provide useful information, especially if you take the time to evaluate them with care. Your review must focus strictly on the actual requirements for job performance. Checking on references is an important part of the evaluation process for serious applicants, even though it may not always be easy to get useful information.

Probably the most important piece of information you can pick up from a resume or job application is the job history. An evaluation grid is a valuable tool to help you measure the candidates' merits in a number of categories.

Chapter Four: Selecting Applicants for Interviews

Objectives

Upon completion of this chapter, you will be able to:

1. **Select from all respondents a group of serious contenders for personal interview.**

2. **Match the skills outlined in resumes and job applications with the skills required in the job description.**

In reviewing resumes and applications, most supervisors and managers prefer some form of the three-pile technique. Let's face it, you can tell during the first reading that some applicants are totally unprepared for the skills the job requires. These applications go into the *no* pile, and a letter should be sent to the applicants thanking them for their interest (more about this letter later). You will also come across some resumes that will make your eyebrows jump— these people have some impressive skills that you could really use in your credit union. These resumes go into the *yes* pile, to be set aside and scheduled for an interview.

The rest of the resumes, as you might expect, go in the maybe pile. The size of this pile will vary, depending on the size of the other piles. If you get no yes candidates, your *maybe* pile will be larger. If you have a thick pile of yes resumes, and you should be so lucky, your maybe pile will shrink.

Recall that the standard you're using is the job description you have just reviewed and possibly rewritten. This document, as interpreted by your experience, determines whom you will ask to come in for an interview.

Use the resume and the job application to structure the actual interview. Many books on job interviewing written for those being interviewed encourage the applicant to steer the questions toward areas of strength. Your job is to resist this and use the interview to fill the gaps in the written materials, answer any questions you might have, and *then* give the applicant the chance to show his or her stuff.

Focus on just what qualities are needed for the job. Do you have a mental image of the perfect candidate? Most employers do. What portions of that mental picture are really needed to perform the job? Are you openminded enough to fairly assess the real people you will be interviewing? Recall what you learned in the exit interview.

Do you have a bias that your candidate has to be attractive? Are you—illegally—looking for someone in his or her early twenties? Won't an older person be able to do the job just as well? If an applicant confesses to you in the interview that he had been convicted of a shoplifting misdemeanor five years ago, does that automatically mean they are out of contention for the job? What do you say in response to the candidate? You must be extremely careful.

What will be your reaction when an applicant rolls into the interview in a wheelchair? What if the applicant is 100 pounds overweight? What if the applicant seems to have the basic skills and appears very quick on his or her feet, but lacks the kind of work experience you would like to see in the position? Letting any of these issues influence your hiring decision could lead to a lawsuit. You need to know local, state, and federal discrimination laws and any other laws or regulations which affect your hiring decision.

Never underestimate the importance of vitality— a can-do spirit with lots of spunk.

Although you may have concerns about the potential for drug or alcohol abuse, it's not something you can explore directly in the hiring process. Alcohol and prescription drugs are, in fact, legal. And the American with Disabilities Act prohibits you from discriminating against people who are currently *not* using drugs illegally, but have completed or are in the middle of drug or alcohol counseling or treatment.

In the hiring process, there's little you can do to identify potential problems like this unless the individual volunteers the information. You can't draw negative conclusions from gaps in resumes.

Don't commit the insecure manager's error of hiring people like yourself, or less powerful than yourself. When you look at an applicant with an open mind, you may be happily surprised.

An employee satisfactory in every aspect may be outstanding in none. You may not come across the dream candidate. What do you do then?

Do you want a brilliant bookkeeper who's a klutz in dealing with people, or a pretty good bookkeeper who's pretty good in dealing with people. These are the tradeoffs you will need to make in hiring in the real world of the work force. You will be far better off opting for adequacy in the portions of the job description that are of secondary importance, and searching for superiority in those parts of the description that are truly important. You will need to live with some imperfections. Choose those imperfections in areas of secondary importance.

Never underestimate the importance of vitality—a can-do spirit with lots of spunk. Training can transmit job skills; education can sharpen the mind. But there is nothing that can create the kind of energy we see and admire in our most vital employees. And that energy, properly directed by management, can lead to major achievement.

Activity 4.1

Write a letter inviting your final candidates to an interview.

You have reviewed all the applications and resumes and decided you want to interview four people for the job as teller. Write a letter to each of the four, including the following information:
- When and where the interview will be held
- How to get there, where to park, how to find you
- Who will be doing the interviewing
- The purpose and expected length of the interview
- Any specific areas you intend to cover
- Any specific paperwork you need them to bring to the interview
- Your interest in answering their questions about your credit union

Be sure your letter is friendly and informative. Don't, however, make the mistake of giving the applicant the impression that she is already likely to get the job.

Dear _____,

_____

_____

_____

_____

_____

_____

_____

_____

_____

_____

_____

_____

_____

_____

_____

_____

_____

_____

_____

_____

_____

_____

_____

_____

_____

Figure 4.1 Sample "Invitation to Interview" Letter

Dear Mr. Jensen,

Thank you for applying for our bookkeeper position. I have reviewed your application and resume, and I would like you to come in for an interview.

Let me suggest two separate times, and you can call and let Jan (264-7363) know which would be best for you.

Wednesday, June 11, at 2:30 p.m.
Thursday, June 12, at 11:45 a.m.

Our main office is 2314 West Kennedy. You can park across the street in the municipal lot. Our first-floor receptionist will guide you to the interviewing office. Allow about fifteen minutes to get to us from the east side of town. I will be doing the interviewing, as this position reports directly to me. I want to review your educational and work background and ask you a few questions. I am particularly interested in your experience the last two years at the Lightex Corporation. It sounds interesting. The interview shouldn't take more than forty-five minutes.

Please bring with you any letters of recommendation or reference you have. At the end of the interview, I will be happy to answer any questions you have about this institution or the specific job opening you're interviewing for.

Please give us a call by the end of the week regarding the interview time. If there are any difficulties, please contact me personally. I look forward to seeing you soon.

Sincerely,
James Pearson
Branch Manager

Summary

In reviewing resumes and applications, you must be objective and you must adhere to the details of the job description. Work to overcome any personal biases. You can't expect all candidates to be outstanding in every area you want. Be prepared to make compromises. Limit the number of candidates you will interview.

Chapter Five: Preparing for the Interview

The most important environmental issues for an employment interview are privacy and lack of interruptions. If you allow your interview to be interrupted by other employees, telephone calls, or members, you are going to lose track of the information you need to gather. You are also sending a *terrible* message to the applicant: You are not someone I take seriously, and I will speak to you about working here only if nothing else takes me away.

After a few interruptions, any applicant with confidence and self-esteem would probably tell you they wouldn't want to work for a company that treats its potential employees this way. If a company can't put on its best face while hiring a new employee, when *will* it get its act together?

If there is the possibility of a brief, absolutely unavoidable interruption during the interview, let the applicant know, and apologize beforehand.

Phone calls can be especially interrupting. Have them forwarded. If the phone on your desk or in the conference room must ring, disconnect it for the course of the interview.

You should be ready to meet the applicant and begin the interview promptly at the appointed time. Keeping a job candidate waiting is unkind. It raises anxiety and gets the interview experience off on the wrong foot. Take care to set aside the right amount of time for the interview. While there are no absolutes in this area, an hour appears to be a reasonable time for a basic employment interview.

Consider some of the other logistical items. How is the noise level in the place you've selected for the interview? Are there intrusive sounds from photocopying machines or vending machines? Is there much foot traffic? How audible are the conversations of others? A quiet location produces the most comfortable and most informative interview.

Seating arrangements for the interview should be flexible. If possible, avoid the "boss behind the desk" position. While this does indeed establish your authority, it may well increase the tension in the situation. And if you expect the applicant to speak frankly to you, you need to make the physical situation as comfortable as possible.

Objectives

Upon completion of this chapter, you will be able to:

1. **Establish a productive environment for the interview.**

2. **Develop an outline of the questions you need to ask each applicant.**

3. **Create a list of custom questions to ask individual applicants.**

4. **Write and review a pre-interview checklist.**

5. **Conduct an interview which takes into account all legal guidelines for hiring.**

Many interviewers speak to applicants away from their own desks, perhaps in a conference room. This greatly reduces the chance of interruption. Of course, for managers who have desks with paper everywhere, conference room interviews allow you the choice of tidying up your desk.

In general, you will want to sit at a table with the applicant, in a place you can spread out the resume, job application, test results (if applicable), and other related papers. Some interviewers prefer working in their own offices, but they won't sit behind the desk. Instead, they will have a small coffee or lounge table in a corner of the office to establish a less formalized interview situation.

Schedule your interviews in the morning if possible. Most people are sharper in the morning, and this also makes it less likely things will come up in your workload that might force you to

cancel or postpone the meeting. Don't schedule more interviews in a row than you can fairly handle. Preparing for the interview will include some obvious and not-so-obvious steps.

1. You have carefully reviewed the applicant's resume and application form and selected this candidate for interview from the pool of applicants. Now you need to develop three sheets of paper for the interview.

   a. A standardized outline, including a sequential list of speaking/listening points. How do you want the interview to go? An interview is often defined as a planned conversation. Make sure you do your planning. Include areas of discussion with specific questions regarding job knowledge/skills, education, and so on.
   This outline should be used for all applicants. You will ask the same questions of each applicant. The answers will reflect the applicant's past experience.

   b. Specific questions based on your review of materials for each candidate. Every resume raises questions. The application will answer some, but not all. You don't want the interview to end with an empty spot in your picture of the candidate. Highlight the facts you *must* get from the candidate in the interview.
   An interview with someone in the workforce for a long time will deal more with

---

Figure 5.1 A Pre-Interview Checklist

☐ • Name
☐ • Address and phone
☐ • Results of position exit interview
☐ • Job description updated
☐ • Resume reviewed
☐ • Applicant testing (if appropriate) and application
☐ • Job application review
☐ • Test results, if appropriate
☐ • Interview time with candidate established
☐ • Interview outline with specific questions prepared
☐ • Evaluation grid
☐ • Room/office prepared and phone calls/interruptions held

job experience, while one with a new graduate will focus more on educational experience.

c. The evaluation grid, discussed earlier. You most likely want to keep this at hand for use during the interview, as you may choose to use some other interview methods and complete the evaluation grid after the actual interview.

2. Make sure you're fully informed on your credit union's benefit package. At the end of the interview, you can expect to be asked questions on the types of insurance coverages that come with the job. This type of question is more likely to be asked by more experienced, more confident candidates. If you appear ignorant or are caught flatfooted by the question, you won't make a very favorable impression. It's simply unprofessional. Most managers are not fully up to speed on the details of coverage. If you're not, get yourself into a briefing by the person on staff most competent in benefits. Better yet, have that person prepare for you a two- or three-page handout which highlights the coverages offered. This handout is for *you*, not the applicant. If you're asked a specific question you can't answer, make a point of having your benefits person call the applicant with the answer on the following day.

3. Consider for a moment the last few people you have interviewed for other jobs in your credit union (assuming this isn't your first interview). Search your mind for just how those interviews progressed, and how good your hiring decision was. Do you see a pattern in your interviewing and hiring decisions? The only way to improve your interviewing technique is to review your track record. A brief review before an upcoming interview can constructively focus your attention on your weaknesses. If this is your first interview, breathe deeply and relax.

4. Double check the details. Check your office and your personal appearance. Make *certain* you have the proper paperwork. Are you certain you won't be interrupted?

5. Take a few minutes to clear your mind and to prepare yourself for the task at hand. Mirror the moment of complete concentration any athlete develops at the moment of challenge. Deciding whether another person becomes a colleague— whether she will contribute to your credit union team or keep looking for a job—is serious business. You should prepare seriously for it.

6. Having relaxed and cleared your mind, now lighten the load—look forward to it with anticipation. Interviewing is tough work on both sides of the equation. You can make it so much easier by adding some simple human warmth and resolving to make it as pleasant an experience as

possible. Don't lose track of your business sense, but don't forget your personal characteristics, such as sympathy, kindness, and humor. If you look toward the approaching interview with dread, the candidate will know it. Your benevolence can make a tense situation much more bearable.

The Legal Framework of the Job Interview

There are many federal, state, and local employment laws regulating what you can and cannot do in the hiring process. This section summarizes only the federal laws. Some state laws place greater restrictions on the hiring process. You should identify a local attorney knowledgeable in this area as a resource. Your state agency charged with administering employment laws should be able to supply you with forms and background information.

Under federal law, you can't discriminate against applicants on the basis of sex, race, religion, age, color, national origin, or disability. This means that, *with very, very limited exceptions,* you can't take these factors into account in any stage of the hiring process. That includes job definition, recruitment, application review, interview selection, interviewing, testing, reference checks, and final decisions. All testing should be exclusively job-related. Tests may face legal challenge if they tend to reject applicants from any protected class in a larger percentage than those in an unprotected class.

The recently-enacted Americans with Disabilities Act creates a special set of responsibilities and restrictions for employers. You must judge whether an applicant is qualified to perform the *essential functions* of a job. These are the fundamental job duties, as opposed to the marginal duties you would like to have filled. A disabled person is qualified for a job if he can perform the essential functions, *with or without reasonable accommodation by the employer.*

Although you can't ask an applicant if he is disabled, you can ask all applicants if there are any areas of the job they can't perform in and what would be required for them to able to do that part of the job. Applicants need not disclose their disabilities if they don't believe an accommodation is needed. You must state you're willing to make reasonable accommodations for qualified applicants.

Your state employment rights agency may provide you with information similar to the following checklist provided by the Wisconsin Division of Equal Rights. This list does not contain all you should know. It's a starting point.

- While you can't ask an applicant's age, you can ask if she is over 18, to comply with state child labor laws.
- While you shouldn't ask about convictions, if you do, you must make it clear that a conviction record is not an automatic bar to employment. If you have special concerns, you may focus on them. For example, you may ask whether the applicant was

Activity 5.1
Test your Legal Sensitivity

For each question, answer D (discriminatory),
ND (non-discriminatory), or S (suspect).

1. _____ When were you born?

2. _____ Have you ever been arrested?

3. _____ Would you be able to work weekends?

4. _____ Do you have any children? How old are they?

5. _____ Are you a citizen of the United States?

6. _____ Have you ever been convicted of a criminal offense?

7. _____ Do you have an established credit rating?

8. _____ Do you have a college degree?

9. _____ What is the color of your hair? Eyes?

10. _____ Have you ever been bonded?

11. _____ Do you have any friends or relatives who work here?

12. _____ Have your wages ever been garnished?

13. _____ Do you have any disabilities that might prevent you from doing this job?

14. _____ How tall are you? How much do you weigh?

15. _____ What is the lowest salary you will accept?

16. _____ What's your maiden name?

17. _____ Are you married?

18. _____ Miss or Mrs.?

19. _____ Are you planning to have children?

20. _____ Have you ever had a different name?

21. _____ Male or female?

22. _____ What is your spouse's name and job?

23. _____ Are you widowed, divorced, or separated?

Answers to these questions are in appendix A at the back of this book.

convicted for a financial crime, like forgery, theft, embezzlement, and so on. If you get positive answers, call your insurer and ask how this affects the bondability of the applicant. Remember your fiduciary duty. But you must also keep in mind that some states prohibit job discrimination based on conviction records unless the conviction is recent, job-related, and you have a reasonable basis to believe there is risk to your credit union. If you get any positive answers, talk to your attorney before making any final decisions.

Asking questions about an applicant's financial history is a different matter and *not* recommended.

- Inquiries about scheduling availability should be asked carefully. Ask only if you *know* the job will require the applicant to work evenings, weekends, etc. Some applicants may have religious prohibitions about working on certain days or at certain times. You must accommodate such practices when they are not an undue hardship.
- Questions about friends or relatives already working for you may appear to imply that you are a "closed shop" and prefer to hire relatives or friends. Minority applicants may perceive this as a method of restricting minority access to your workforce.

This issue may sometimes be viewed in exactly the oppo-

site way. Asking such questions may indicate to an applicant that you have a policy of *not* hiring family members of current employees.

- Questions about personal finance or family situation are not relevant and are discouraged, since they appear to discourage minorities and women. If you're concerned about attendance, tell the applicant the truth—that good attendance is a crucial part of the job. You can't make assumptions regarding how race, sex, age, disability, lifestyle, and other factors will affect the performance of any particular person.

Avoiding "Loaded" Employment Questions which May Lead to Discrimination

This information is reproduced from a pamphlet produced by Wisconsin for use by state employers. It presents a comprehensive look at the issues involved in discrimination, especially in the context on job interviews. Close study will reveal a great deal about the environment in which you're conducting your personnel activities. Your state authorities should be able to provide you with corresponding guidance for your home state. Despite their excellent guidance, these details apply only for Wisconsin.

Employers usually and rightfully ask a number of questions

of applicants for employment to determine who is best qualified for the position(s) available. Many employers aren't aware that some of the traditional questions they ask might be illegal, or interpreted as discriminatory under Wisconsin's Fair Employment Law, or other laws.

Employers should be aware that, when asking such questions, they may be running a risk of encouraging unlawful discrimination by their agents, or providing evidence which may be used by individuals who later complain of discrimination.

Even when the employer does not use the information in the answers, the questions may have the unlawful effect of discouraging individuals from even applying for jobs for which they may be well-qualified.

The key to lawful employment inquiries is to ask only about those areas that will provide information as to the person's ability to do the job, with reasonable accommodation.

It is equally important to remember, however, that this list is concerned only with the potential unlawful use of information. Quite different considerations are involved when the purpose of seeking information is to carry out an affirmative action program. If some of the information discussed here is needed for post-employment information, it can be obtained after the applicant has been selected for employment.

The Equal Rights Division believes it serves citizens best when it works with employers, employees, and
jobseekers to eliminate discrimination before it occurs, wherever possible. That is the reason for this pamphlet, and various other printed materials the agency makes available to the public.

The Division also is willing to answer employers' and employees' questions, even if it poses anonymously by telephone, about interpretation of the anti-discrimination laws and the complaint process itself. Telephone numbers and mailing addresses are listed on the back of this publication. In addition, the Division is willing to provide speakers for educational seminars, at no cost to the sponsoring organizations, as part of this educational effort.

1. Age? Date of birth?

The Wisconsin Fair Employment Law and the Federal Age Discrimination in Employment Act prohibit discrimination on the basis of age. Wisconsin prohibits discrimination on the basis of age against individuals who are age 40 and over, while federal law covers age 40 through 70. Answers to these questions could be used unlawfully.

2. Arrests?

Wisconsin law prohibits inquiries about arrest records. The only arrest record that may be considered is one involving a pending charge. A past arrest that did not lead to a conviction should not be given any consideration since the person was not proven guilty.

If an applicant has a pending arrest that is related to the job to be performed, an employer can suspend judgment until the court decision, if possible, or advise the applicant to reapply when the pending charge has been resolved. An employer should never reject an applicant outright, or discharge an employee, because of a pending arrest.

Federal law does not specifically address arrest records, but covers this area when inquiries about arrests tend to exclude members of particular minority groups. (Also see section 6, Convictions)

3. Available for Saturday or Sunday work?

This question may discourage applications from persons of certain religions which prohibit their adherents from working on Saturday or Sunday. On the other hand, employers may need to know whether an applicant can work on these days.

The Wisconsin Fair Employment Law and Title VII of the Civil Right Act of 1964 both prohibit discrimination on the basis of religion and require accommodation of a person's religious beliefs and practices. Both laws exempt employers from compliance who can demonstrate that they are unable to reasonably accommodate an employee's (or prospective employee's) religious observance without undue hardship on the conduct of the business.

If a question about Saturday or Sunday work is asked, the employer should indicate that a reasonable effort is made to accommodate the religious needs of employees.

4. Children under 18? Age of children? What arrangements will you make for care of minor children?

The purpose of these questions is to explore what the employer believes to be a common source of absenteeism and tardiness. But why explore this area in such an indirect way, and in a way which traditionally applies only to women? There are a number of common causes of absenteeism and tardiness which affect both men and women and which would be worthy of exploration if this is a matter of substantial concern to the employer. In the absence of proof of business necessity, Title VII and Wisconsin law prohibit employers from having one hiring policy for women with pre-school children and another for men with pre-school children.

5. Citizen of what country?

There are federal guidelines on discrimination because of national origin which contain the following statement: "Because discrimination on the basis of citizenship has the effect of discriminating on the basis of national origin, a lawfully immigrated alien who is domiciled or residing in this country may not be discriminated against on the basis of his citizenship," unless national security requirements mandated by a federal statute or executive order authorize otherwise. State and federal courts have recently declared invalid laws in several states which exclude noncitizens from public employment. Both Wisconsin and federal laws prohibit discrimination on the basis of national origin.

In addition, because this question asks of which country the applicant is a citizen, it makes it possible to discriminate on the basis of a particular national origin.

6. Convictions?

The Wisconsin Fair Employment Law prohibits an employer from refusing to employ a person with a conviction record unless the circumstances of the conviction substantially relate to circumstances of the particular job. If the application form makes any inquiry about convictions, it should indicate that a criminal record does not constitute an automatic bar to employment and will be considered only as it relates to the job in question. Further, any person who evaluates information concerning criminal records should be given careful instructions regarding the limited ways in which it may be used.

7. Credit record? (Charge accounts? Own your home? Own your furniture? Own a car?)

Because minority persons, on the average, are poorer than whites, consideration of these factors by employers has an adverse effect on minorities. Answers are almost always irrelevant to performance of the job in question, so information requests of this nature could probably be shown to be unlawful unless clearly required by considerations of business necessity.

8. Educational Background?

While an employer may wish to inquire as to an applicant's educational history, care should be taken that only clearly job-related education is considered

when a hiring decision is made. While a law degree is necessary for a lawyer, there are no positions where a general college degree is a necessary requirement. Rather than asking about a degree or diploma, consideration should be given to how the applicants can actually demonstrate that they have the skills necessary to function in the job.

Consideration of degrees or formal education in making hiring decisions may be unlawful when there is a disparate impact on some groups, such as minorities, and the employer is unable to show the degree or education is necessary for the performance of the job.

9. Eyes? Hair?

Eye color and hair color are not related to the performance of jobs and may serve to indicate an employee's race, religion, or national origin.

10. Fidelity bond ever refused to you?

This question should only be asked when applicants are applying for a position requiring bonding. Even then the information should be used with care, taking into consideration factors such as the length of time since the refusal and the prospective applicant's current bondability.

11. Friends or relatives working with us?

This question may reflect a preference for friends or relatives of present employees. Such a preference would be unlawful if it has the effect of reducing employment opportunities for women and minorities. It would have this unlawful effect if an employer's present work force differs significantly in its proportion of women or minorities from the population of the area from which workers are recruited. This question may also reflect a rule that only one partner in a marriage can work for an employer. There is a growing recognition that such a rule hurts women far more often than men and that the rule serves no necessary business purpose.

Under the current interpretations of discrimination on the basis of marital status, it is illegal to refuse to hire someone because that person's spouse works for the same employer. It would not be illegal to refuse to hire if one spouse would directly supervise the other, however.

12. Garnishment record?

This question could have a tendency to exclude members of some groups. For example, courts have found that minorities have wages garnished substantially more often than whites, and that wage garnishments do not affect a worker's ability to effectively perform assigned work.

13. Handicapped?

The Wisconsin Fair Employment Law defines a handicapped individual as someone who has, or is perceived to have, a physical or mental handicap which makes achievement unusually difficult, or limits the capacity to work.

Under this law, an employer is also required to accommodate a handicapped employee's special needs, unless it causes undue hardship to the employer's business.

If the employer makes any inquiry as to a person's health status, the inquiry should be clearly relevant to the work to be performed and employers should make known their willingness to accommodate.

14. Height? Weight?

Some employers impose minimum height and weight requirements for employees that are not related to the job to be performed and which exclude above-average percentages of women and members of certain nationality groups. Weight and height may be a protected handicap under state law.

15. Honesty testing? Are honesty tests required as part of the employment application process?

Hiring decisions may not be based on the results of a polygraph test, without the employer considering additional relevant information he has obtained independently. Wisconsin law further requires the employer to use only one permitted type of mechanical device that visually, permanently, and simultaneously records the person's cardiovascular and respiratory patterns and changes. The applicant must voluntarily submit and the applicant must be so informed in writing and orally. Questions asked must be related to the person's performance or conduct in past or present employment.

16. Lowest salary will accept?

Women generally have held poorer paying jobs than men, and have been paid less than men for the same work. As a result of these past practices, a woman might be willing to work for less pay than a man would find acceptable. It is unlawful, however, to pay a woman less than a male employee who is or was performing the same or similar work.

17. Maiden Name?

This is not relevant to a person's ability to perform a job and could be used for a discriminatory purpose. For example, a woman's maiden name might be used as an indication of her religion or national origin. This item also constitutes an inquiry into marital status which is discussed in the next section.

18. Marital Status?

The Wisconsin Fair Employment Law specifically prohibits discrimination based on marital status. Marital status is defined as the state of being married, single, divorced, separated, or widowed. It would violate both Wisconsin and federal law, for example, for an employer to refuse to hire a married woman or pay a married woman less than a married man for the same work because of the belief that the woman's pay represents a second family income while men's pay does not. Finally, an employer could not refuse to hire a person for any job or for particular jobs because of the employer's beliefs concerning morality, parental or family responsibility, or because that person's spouse already works for the employer.

19. Mr., Miss, or Mrs.?

This is simply another way of asking the applicant's sex and (for women only) marital status, both of which are irrelevant.

20. Pregnant? Planning on having children?

Any employer may not refuse to hire a woman, under both Wisconsin and federal employment laws, because she is or might become pregnant. To ask this question only increases the likelihood of the employer being charged with discrimination, even if a decision not to hire was made on some other basis.

21. Prior Name?

An employer might ask if a person has used a different name in previous employment so that the employer can check references. Although traditionally only women have changed their names upon marriage, the agent for the employer should be instructed not to make assumptions about the reasons for the person's change of name.

22. Sex?

Wisconsin Fair Employment Law and Title VII prohibit discrimination on the basis of sex except in very few instances in which sex may be a "bonafide occupational qualification reasonably necessary to the normal operation" of the employer's business. There are virtually no jobs which can be performed by only one sex.

23. Spouse's Name?

To the extent that this question asks for marital status, the comments on marital status apply. A spouse's name may also be used as an indication of religion or national origin.

24. Spouse's Work?

To the extent that this question also asks for marital status, the comments on marital status apply. In addition, some employers have been reluctant to hire a woman if that would make her the second breadwinner in the family, while there is seldom any objection to hiring a man if that would make him the second family breadwinner. Such a policy is unlawful under Wisconsin law and Title VII.

25. Widowed, divorced, or separated?

Again, marital status is an illegal basis for a hiring decision. In addition, recent statistics show that many more black than white persons are either widowed, divorced, or separated and that a much larger proportion of women than men in the labor force is either widowed, divorced, or separated. Thus, this question has a potential for adversely affecting women and blacks.

Your credit union should establish guidelines on conducting non-discriminating interviews. As you saw in figure 1.1, the Sample Policy for Job Openings, Recruitment and Selection included a section on conducting non-discriminating interviews. We have provided this section of the policy in figure 5.2 for your review.

Summary

Take the time to make the interview setting comfortable and quiet. For each interview, you should have a standardized outline, a list of questions you will ask each candidate, some specific questions for the individual candidate, and your evaluation grid. A pre-interview checklist will help to keep you organized when dealing with a number of interviews.

All hiring takes place in a complex legal environment. Spare no efforts to familiarize yourself with federal and state guidelines in interviewing and hiring.

Figure 5.2 Additional Guidelines for Conducting Non-Discriminatory Interviews

Policy #302
Eff 11-1-91
Page 4 of 6

GUIDELINES FOR CONDUCTING NON-DISCRIMINATORY INTERVIEWS

Subject:

Name

Lawful Inquiries: Is any additional information relative to change of name, use of an assumed name, or nickname necessary to enable a check on your work record? If yes, explain.

Unlawful Inquiries: What is your original name? (Applicant whose name has been changed by court order or otherwise; or maiden name of a married woman.) Have you ever worked under another name?

Marital &
Family
Status

Lawful Inquiries: Can you meet specified work schedules? Do you have activities, commitments or responsibilities that may hinder the meeting of work attendance requirements?

Unlawful Inquiries: Are you married, single, divorced, engaged, etc? How many children do you have? What are their ages? Are you pregnant? Do you plan on having a family? (Any such questions which directly or indirectly might result in limitation of job opportunity in any way. If an applicant is pregnant they cannot be denied the job just because they are pregnant.) What are your marriage plans? What does your spouse do? What happens if your spouse gets transferred or needs to relocate? Who will take care of your child while you are at work?

References

Lawful: By whom were you referred for a position here? Can you give me the names of persons willing to provide professional and/or character references for you? Who suggested that you apply for a position here?

Unlawful: Require the submission of a religious reference. Request reference from applicant's pastor.

Age

Lawful: Are you under the age of 18?

Unlawful: How old are you? What is your date of birth? How would you feel working for a person younger than you?

Sex

Lawful: No questions should be asked relating to this subject.

Unlawful: A pre-employment inquiry as to sex on an application form shall be unlawful. Do not ask a man how he would feel working for a woman or vice versa.

Figure 5.2 Additional Guidelines for Conducting Non-Discriminatory Interviews   *page 2*

Policy #302
Eff 11-1-91
Page 5 of 6

Race or Color	Lawful: No questions should be asked relating to this subject.
	Unlawful: Complexion or color of skin. Coloring. Do you feel that your sex/race/color will be a problem in your performing your job?
Ancestry or National Origin	Lawful: What languages do you read, speak or write fluently?
	Unlawful: What is your lineage, ancestry, national origin, descent, birthplace, or mother tongue? What is the national origin of parents or spouse?
Religion	Lawful: No questions should be asked relating to this subject.
	Unlawful: What is your religious denomination, religious affiliations, church, parish, pastor, or religious holidays observed? An applicant may not be told, "This is a (Catholic, Protestant, or Jewish) organization." Do you hold any religious beliefs that would prevent you from working certain days of the week?
Address or Duration of Residence	Lawful: What is your address? How long a resident of this state or city?
	Unlawful: Specific inquiry into foreign addresses which would indicate national origin. What are the names or relationship of persons with whom you reside? Do you own or rent a home?
Military Record	Lawful: What education and experience did you have in the service that relates to the job you are interviewing for?
	Unlawful: What type of discharge did you receive? Did you receive a dishonorable discharge?
Education	Lawful: What academic, vocational or professional education and private or public schools have you attended? What is the highest grade you completed?
	Unlawful: Why did you attend? Did you receive loans or aids for education? How much? What year did you graduate from high school?
Character	Lawful: Have you ever been convicted of a crime? If so, when, where and what is the disposition of your offense?
	Unlawful: Have you ever been arrested? (An employer's use of an individual's arrest record to deny employment would, in the absence of business necessity, constitute a violation of the fair employment laws.)

Figure 5.2 Additional Guidelines for Conducting Non-Discriminatory Interviews   *page 3*

Policy #302
Eff 11-1-91
Page 6 of 6

Relatives   <u>Lawful:</u> Do you have any relatives already employed by us?

                                   <u>Unlawful:</u> What are the names, addresses, ages, number or other information concerning applicant's children or other relatives not employed by the company.

Credit   <u>Lawful:</u> Nothing unless specific business requirements can be shown.
Rating   When specifically job related circumstances apply, indicate that a credit check will be done and ask if they will have any objections to this. Tell them they will be advised of any negative information which causes their rejection and the source of this information.

                                   <u>Unlawful:</u> Any questions concerning credit rating, charge accounts, etc. Not advising an applicant when a negative report contributes to their rejection. Refusing to divulge the source of negative credit information.

Chapter Six: The Interview

Perhaps the most important fact about interviews you should keep in mind is that most candidates would rather be at the dentist. Most of us see interviews as a necessary, but brutal, trial by fire through which we must pass to qualify for a desirable position.

As an interviewer, you have two jobs: to learn any job-related information regarding the candidate that doesn't appear in the application or resume, and to assess and evaluate the information in relation to the job requirements and in relation to the other candidates. These two tasks are the only reason you're in the room with the candidate.

Every interview is unique, but we can also say they are all the same. People who have done thousands of interviews suggest a basic structure to lead you and the candidate through the hurdles quickly and gracefully.

1. Start with a warm and sincere greeting. Applicants deserve courtesy and professional treatment, and professional treatment quickly establishes two facts: this is the way we do business around here—friendly and sincere. The prospective employee realizes you feel she is important enough to take some time with.

   Get out of your chair and greet the candidate with a firm handshake, directing her to the appropriate seat. If you are the one charged with

Objectives

Upon completion of this chapter, you will be able to:

1. **Conduct an interview sensitive to the tension created by the interview situation.**

2. **Make a candidate comfortable while still obtaining the answers to the questions developed in the pre-interview stage.**

3. **Review work and educational experience with the candidate.**

4. **Ask open-ended questions to encourage the candidate to reveal himself.**

5. **Consider the use of testing and assessment techniques to provide additional applicant information.**

6. **Finish the interview with detailed notes to serve as a documentary resource for decision-making and legal support.**

---

bringing the candidate to your office, you can start with some social small talk en route to ease the situation.

2. Reduce the anxiety with some small talk—weather, traffic, parking, and so on. A tense candidate is not going to speak comfortably about anything. Your aim in the earliest minutes of the interview is to develop a comfortable tone and atmosphere. Make the candidate see you're not an ogre.

   This is the appropriate time to arrange something for the candidate to drink. Talking

---

A tense candidate is not going to speak comfortably about anything.

---

about yourself can create quite a thirst. Offer coffee, ice water, or a soft drink. This refreshment will keep the applicant from drying up from tension. It also provides him or her with something to keep the hands busy. In tense situations, it's always nice to have a diversion.

In your small talk, take care that you don't wander into any of the areas you can't legally speak about in an employment interview. Avoid personal questions that lead into legally questionable territory. In the interview situation, you are just as vulnerable as the candidate. Don't spend more than a few minutes before getting on with the interview.

3. Start the interview proper with a brief statement about the position. You don't want to go through an entire interview only to find out the applicant thought the position was part-time, or that he was hoping to start in the position in three months, after the summer, or that the applicant has had some second thoughts about working in the financial field.

Begin with distinct and concise summary: "Well, Elizabeth, you're here to interview for our position of full-time bookkeeper. Thank you for coming." This is clear and unambiguous. If your candi-

date has reservations, now is the time you will hear them. Using the applicant's name adds a bit of a personal touch. You are showing the applicant you consider them to be more than a piece of paper.

As you make notes during the interview, make sure you let the candidate know what you're doing and that you make such notes during all interviews. This will reduce the applicant's tension as you start to make your notes. Figure 6.1 provides a worksheet for tracking information during the interview.

4. Make an overview statement explaining how the interview will proceed. Rather than have the interview format loom as a great and frightful unknown for the candidate, reveal your strategy immediately. This will let the applicant know what's coming, and it will help to establish a pace for the interview itself. It will also remove temptation on the part of the applicant to discuss issues more properly dealt with later in the program.

When you put together this statement, include some detail about the individual application so the candidate knows you have already looked closely at his or her materials. Finally, let the applicant know approximately how long you expect the interview to last.

5. Go through the applicant's job experience. Most interviewers go through the last two or three jobs in some detail. While there's no value

Figure 6.1 A Sample Interview Worksheet

Purpose	Notes from Job Requirements, Application, etc.	Questions to Ask and Information to Give	Notes from Interview
A. Warm up and establish control.		Introduce self and shake hands. Indicate where to sit. Offer coffee or tea. Explain how interview will proceed. Brief "small talk," such as weather, did you have any trouble getting here, etc.	
B. Can the candidate do the job? Screen candidate eligibility in regard to job knowledge, skills, experience, and physical demands.	Have a job description available. Check all requirements carefully with candidate. Have candidate's application & resume available and probe previous job activities and training to determine actual abilities.	Describe the job requirements. Ask direct questions to probe abilities as demonstrated in previous work experience as reported on application, such as: How is your previous work experience applicable to this job? What were your duties and responsibilities? Which were the most difficult for you? What are your greatest strengths? Give me an example from your previous job. Tell me the kinds of equipment you can operate and describe your level of skill.	

THE INTERVIEW

Figure 6.1 A Sample Interview Worksheet–*continued*   *page 2*

Purpose	Notes from Job Requirements, Application, etc.	Questions to Ask and Information to Give	Notes from Interview
C. Will the candidate do the job? Ascertain candidate's willingness to meet performance, behavior, and attendance standards.	Followed directions in completing the application.	Ask open-ended questions, such as: Is there anything that would prevent you from meeting the work schedule I've described? How many days were you absent from work in the past year? How would you describe the rules where you worked before? What kind of work do you enjoy most? What is the most difficult thing for you to do in a job? How do you deal with that? Give me an example of a specific situation and how you handled it.	On time for interview? Dress and grooming appropriate?
D. How will the candidate get along with others? Probe candidate's willingness and ability to work cooperatively and effectively within the existing work climate and team of employees.		Ask open-ended questions, such as: What did you like about your previous job? If you could change one thing about your previous work situation what would it be? Describe your ideal supervisor. Describe your previous supervisor. What kind of working relationship do you typically have with your co-workers? If I asked your former co-workers to describe you, what would they say? What is the best way to handle an angry member who is being rude to you?	Polite to receptionist? Listens when you talk? Cooperates in the interview?

Figure 6.1 A Sample Interview Worksheet–*continued*   *page 3*

Purpose	Notes from Job Requirements, Application, etc.	Questions to Ask and Information to Give	Notes from Interview
E. Is the job of interest to the candidate?		**DON'T OVERSELL OR MAKE PROMISES.**	
Communicate clearly to the candidate the positives and negatives about the job, working conditions, and the organization.		What are concerns you have about the job? How do you work under pressure?	

in asking what's clearly stated in the paperwork, this is a good time for an open-ended question on what the applicant liked or disliked about these recent work experiences. You might also ask what a typical workday was like, or how busy the work became at certain times of the year.

Job experience is the most important thing the candidate will bring to you. Make certain you understand it thoroughly. When you looked at the candidate's resume and application in your office, you developed some questions about his or her work history. Now's the best time to ask them. Make certain you have satisfied yourself about the applicant's work history before you move on to other parts of the interview.

6. Review the applicant's educational background. If the applicant's educational background ends at high school, this will

be a brief part of the interview. When there's more education involved, use open-ended questions to reveal more about the candidate than gradepoint averages and biology courses. Ask about any business or accounting courses. If the applicant has had some distributive education experience, such as a business school co-op program, learn all you can about it.

Figure 6.2 A Sample Overview Statement

"I expect we'll be talking for about an hour, Barbara. What I would like to do first is go through some of the experience you mentioned in your application, particularly your work for the past three years at the Excelsior Corporation and your summer work at the First National Bank of Jerseyside. Once I understand the details of your work experience, I would like you to tell me about your educational experience, especially what types of courses you took in your associate degree work. Please don't forget to fill me in on that project you led for the Jaycees.
After that, we will fill in a few factual details I need to complete your application. Then I would like you to tell me what you know about this credit union and this job in particular. That's my plan for today. What do you say we get started?"

7. Make certain all ambiguities are cleared up. In preparing your interview outline, you had some gaps to fill. By this time in the interview, you should have covered each of them. But make sure. Take a moment before moving on to the next portion of the interview. There's no better time than now to ask this applicant a question.

8. Ask for questions. Some interviewers get so caught up in their own information-gathering task, they forget the candidate may have some questions, too. Many candidates will not. They may not want to appear presumptuous by asking questions about a job they haven't yet been offered.

   Other candidates will have questions. And those questions are often very revealing. If your candidate asks about nothing but salary, raises, and benefits, you know you're dealing with someone moti-vated by money. If the questions deal with promotion and the chances for increased responsibility, then you have someone who's mission-oriented, or at least who wants to appear mission-oriented. Make a note of the types of questions asked. If you are asked something you don't know, get back to the candidate over the phone.

9. Conclude with future steps (notification of results, etc.). Let the applicant know roughly when you expect to make a decision, and that you will contact her either through a phone call or letter. Thank the applicant for his or her time and interest. When you are finished, you should give the candidate a warm handshake and walk her to the front door of the credit union. Now's your second chance for some relaxing small talk.

Interview Techniques

People are complicated, and no two interviews are ever going to follow the same route. Here are some guidelines developed by business management and personnel specialists that can make your job easier.

You don't need to feel that with each interview you're forced to enter unexplored territory without guideposts. You should develop a familiarity with the following interview techniques. They will allow you to conduct more relaxed, productive, and complete interviews.

Figure 6.3 Basic Interview Structure

1. Start with a warm and sincere greeting.
2. Reduce the anxiety with some small talk.
3. Start the interview proper with a brief statement about the position.
4. Make an overview statement explaining how the interview will proceed.
5. Go through the applicant's job experience.
6. Review the applicant's educational background.
7. Make certain all ambiguities are cleared up.
8. Ask for questions.
9. Conclude with future steps (notification of results, etc.).

General Interview Techniques

1. The applicant should do 80 percent of the talking. Rarely will you have as captive an audience as when you're interviewing someone for a job at your credit union. This person has every reason in the world to find all you say charming and insightful. Some interviewers find this power a heady experience and they talk much more than they should.

   Recall that your goal in conducting the interview is to draw the candidate out, to get him to reveal the inner self and to fill in blanks on personal background. Avoid the temptation to expound on your theory of credit unions or to present your analysis of current events.

   At the same time, you will have some candidates that are unbridled talkers. To deal with this situation and to help you get through your list of questions, simply preface your open-ended questions with a phrase like "Briefly, tell me what was behind your decision to go to school in Canada" or "In just a minute or two, fill me in on your work on the new legislation." If you say this with conviction, your applicant will get the message. But *don't* become a clock-watcher; this will simply aggravate the problem and increase the tension level.

2. Learn the value of the calculated pause. There will be times in every interview when things bog down for a moment. Perhaps it's a time of transition from work experience to educational background. Perhaps you have just probed into a past gap in employment and received a vague answer. Use silence as a technique to get the applicant to break the silence with additional information. The silence, even if it runs to six seconds, can create a positive tension which can result in valuable information. During the pause, move your glance from the applicant's face to your notes and back again. Don't stare.

3. Speak at the applicant's language level; don't use trade talk. You are likely to be better trained and educated than most of your applicants. This is especially true when you are hiring for lower-level positions. Your task is not to intimidate the applicant with your vocabulary. Make an effort to give the applicant a "user-friendly" time. Keep your sentences short and simple. Use common words. If you use a credit union term (such as *members*), explain it clearly the first time you use it.

4. Act as a facilitator for the applicant. Over the course of an hour-long interview, it's likely the candidate is going to talk himself into a corner. Perhaps a train of thought will go astray. A question will be forgotten. Consider it your task to support the applicant in revealing what you want to know. Refresh the candidate's memory when it fails. Ask a question again if it might

THE INTERVIEW

prove helpful. It's tough work talking about yourself for the better part of an hour. You can help.

5. Don't settle for the positive. If your job interview turns up nothing negative, it hasn't been a good interview. We all have negatives in our background. We have skill weaknesses, perhaps in math or English. We have had jobs where we haven't done as well as we might have. Part of your job is to uncover these weaknesses. We're not talking about breaking down a personality; it's simply a matter of understanding the person.

    Life is a collection of trade-offs. If we want a car that offers the utmost in luxury and gives us the quietest drive possible, we have to be prepared to trade off good gas mileage, and to pay a high purchase price. It's no different with people. Each of us has strengths and weaknesses. And no one can truly know us who has no sense of our weaknesses.

Don't trust your memory. Use a notepad and jot notes throughout the interview.

One of the standard interview questions is to ask the candidate "What are your major weaknesses?" Often, you won't get truthful answers to this question. But it's still an important question to ask. Not only will such a question give you some raw material to ana-lyze about the candidate, it also presents evidence as to how self-aware the candidate is — how honest he is with himself about personal weaknesses.

6. Take notes, lots of notes. If you interview more than three or four people, you're soon going to start mixing up details. Unless you take interview notes, you're restricted to resumes, applications, references, and your memory. Don't trust your memory. Use an evaluation grid like those shown in chapter 3 or a notepad and jot notes throughout the interview. Include notes to assist you at a later time in evaluating the candidate. If you have ever tried to reconstruct the content of a business meeting when you have lost your notes, you know how difficult it can be.

    Be consistent in your note taking for all applicants. It's advisable to use a form like an evaluation grid to make your notes. Using a form helps keep the interviewing process fair for all applicants.

    Make your note taking as unobtrusive as possible. If the candidate feels you're simply transcribing what's being said, he may simply stop speaking openly. You may keep the pad in your lap rather than on top of the table or desk. Don't write from beginning to end in the interview, but make notes which will remind you of revealing statements. Don't write your notes the moment the applicant says something noteworthy. Wait a few moments.

Otherwise you will make them nervous about saying the wrong thing.

Never let your note taking cause you to lose overall eye contact with the candidate. Remember how distressing it was in school when a teacher would simply *read* the lecture? Don't make the same mistake. Keep up the personal contact. If the applicant gets into a stressful interlude, perhaps talking about a difficult time in school, or a serious problem at a previous job, stop writing until the incident is over.

After the candidate leaves the interview, you can take a few minutes to review your notes and add any details you need. These interview notes will prove invaluable when it's time for you to sit down and make your hiring decision.

7. Don't let the candidate be surprised by a negative decision. Let's assume for a moment that you are going to interview eight candidates for a position. Chances are, by the time you are halfway through each of the interviews, you're going to have a strong sense that two of the candidates are serious contenders, two have no chance, and four will take some further thought.

In your reaction to a candidate's answers to your questions, or in your response to questions from the candidate, don't raise false hopes just because you want to be kind. If you say something like: "Well, Betty, I certainly think you're one of the very top peo-

ple I've talked to for this position," the candidate is going to feel very confident about her job chances. That's really not appropriate unless you are very sure Betty's going to get the job. But if you're saying it to someone who has no realistic chance of the job, you are actually being cruel while trying to be gentle.

The people you interview aren't fools. They are looking for signs from you, especially at the end of the interview. Be especially careful at the conclusion of the interview to avoid raising false hopes by an overly-positive comment. Keep your own counsel. Explain that you're interviewing a number of people for the job. Make no commitments, give no hope for positive outcomes. You are simply going to talk with all candidates and then make your decision.

8. Does interview behavior form a pattern with education and employment? One of the things you should be looking for in the interview is a unity of impression. You have undoubtedly formed an initial impression of the candidate based on resume and application. After all, you have already decided the applicant is qualified enough for an interview. How would you characterize the candidate's personality based on the paperwork, and what do you see in the interview?

Does someone with a solid educational and employment record seem disciplined and mature in the interview? Is a spotty record in school reflected in an immature and joking attitude in the job interview? If there's a clash between the paper person and the interview person, the interview person is probably more accurate, once the effects of nervousness are taken into account.

9. Pay attention to body language, but don't get carried away. There are entire books devoted to the details of body positioning and what it tells you about people. Most of us recognize that someone sitting across from us with legs crossed tightly, arms crossed over the chest, and a scowl on the face is not responding positively to what we're saying. If you see your applicant fidgeting nervously and sweating, increase your efforts to make him comfortable. You should be a little concerned about a candidate that won't look you in the eye when answering your questions. Nervousness can make people a little afraid of looking directly at an authority figure, which you are. As the nerves settle down, you should see more eye-to-eye contact.

Don't get too caught up in nonverbal language. After all, you've only known this person for a few minutes. You're pretty presumptuous to think you can make too much of the way she sits, folds the arms, or makes facial expressions.

You have your own body language as well, and the candidate may be very aware of it. Don't doodle on your notepad. Don't clean your nails

with your pen or a paper clip. You would be shocked to know how many people do this in meetings. Make sure you're maintaining strong concentration and major eye contact. Don't get caught with your attention wandering as you gaze at the clouds passing by outside the window. If your applicant is observant, he will recognize you are not doing your job in this interview. This gives a bad impression and the applicant may feel this isn't the kind of place she wants to work.

10. Keep an open mind for the duration of the interview. One study of job interviewers revealed that most of them had made their decision in the first quarter of the interview. This isn't good. The least you can do, out of respect for the candidate and out of recognition of the complexities of judging people, is to suspend judgment through the interview. Don't rush to make a decision. While it's true that a weak handshake or a mumbling habit at the opening of the interview may trigger a negative response, these behaviors don't necessarily reveal a significant personal deficiency. We talked earlier about the halo effect, where an interviewer is swayed in a candidate's favor by a big positive, while ignoring substantial negative factors.

If the candidate shows up for the interview without a tie, that might speak to an ignorance of business custom, but it shouldn't destroy any chance of getting the job.

Keep all your options open until you have had a chance to speak with all candidates and review all the materials in the quiet of your office. Only then should you push yourself to make yes/no judgments.

Don't let your personal likes and dislikes interfere with the objectivity of the hiring process. If you're an avid sports fan and an applicant tells you that he thinks sports are a waste of time, don't argue or let the comment affect your hiring decision. Remember, you're not hiring a friend, you are hiring an employee for a particular job.

Don't make up your mind in the course of the interview that candidate Whitman is going to be your new employee. You will lose your concentration during the rest of the interviews. And you may offer Whitman the job, only to be turned down. Then you're handicapped in your evaluation of the rest of the candidates because you would have already written them off.

11. Don't take advantage of your position. As the interviewer /hirer, you're in a position of power. Don't ask questions that you have no right to know. If a person volunteers that he is just recently divorced, don't ask what happened or whether the person is dating yet. Don't make inquiries about issues in which you may have a natural curiosity, but which have nothing to do with the business at hand. Remember your legal boundaries.

12. Stay fresh. Avoid going on automatic pilot. Interviewing is strenuous work. And even the best interviewers must challenge themselves to maintain a high energy level. If you're interviewing a significant number of people for the same position, you're liable to come to feel you have heard it all before. You may find your attention wandering. Your questioning may become half-hearted. You may drift from your outline and let a candidate ramble on more than you should.

There's no simple cure for this *interview boredom.* All you can do is be aware of the problem and fight against it. Don't schedule more than two interviews in a row, or more than four in a day. Get away from your desk between interviews and walk into the lobby or through the back office. This staleness is a real danger in interviewing. Don't ignore it.

13. Be an active listener. Show your interest in the candidate by listening intently to everything he is saying. That means keeping your note taking from getting in the way of your concentration. You should be responding with the little expressions we all use to show someone we understanding what's being said:

"I see what you mean."
"That makes sense."
"I follow you."
"Okay."

While these expressions may appear artificial and a little insincere on a printed page like this, they make up an important part of what humans call conversation. The next time you listen to a friend, give her no response of any kind and see how long it takes to provoke a response. And it probably won't be a positive one.

We can all tell when someone is truly listening to us and when we are just being tolerated. Make every effort to pay attention and *look like* you are paying attention to your applicant's comments.

Figure 6.4 General Interview Techniques

1. The applicant should do 80 percent of the talking.
2. Learn the value of the calculated pause.
3. Speak at the applicant's language level; don't use trade talk.
4. Act as a facilitator for the applicant.
5. Don't settle for the positive.
6. Take notes, lots of notes.
7. Don't let the candidate be surprised by a negative decision.
8. Does interview behavior form a pattern with education and employment?
9. Pay attention to body language, but don't get carried away.
10. Keep an open mind for the duration of the interview.
11. Don't take advantage of your position.
12. Stay fresh. Avoid going on automatic pilot.
13. Be an active listener.

Asking Questions

1. Ask open-ended questions. Unless you want to spend most of the interview thinking up questions to ask, you should get into the habit of asking open-ended questions, questions that cannot be answered by a simple yes or no. Answering open-ended questions demands a differ-

ent type of involvement from the candidate. Recall your own experience in school, when you were probably praying for a multiple choice test in English, rather than the dreaded essay questions, where you really had to reveal what you knew.

Open-ended questions let the candidate reveal himself. They put the candidate in charge of the information shared, and you get a chance to see how the candidate's mind works. Does the applicant show considerable intellectual ability, or are the responses limited to a surface understanding of the job? Does the candidate demonstrate an honest self-knowledge? Does he show a fluency with the language? Does the answer really address your question, or does the candidate wander aimlessly?

One problem with open-ended questions you should be aware of—some people will react negatively and bounce it back to you with phrases such as, "What would you like to know about the time I spent in the entertainment business?" Put the burden back on their shoulders by asking them to tell you what *they* think is appropriate for you to know about their experiences. Such a verbal tactic forces them to make the kind of intellectual and emotional decisions you want them to make.

Your interview, along with the rest of the application materials, should provide you a full picture of the candidate's skills and aptitudes. The way you ask open-ended questions, and the way the candidate responds to them, can reveal the *person*.

Even if you ask open-ended questions, your part isn't done. Respondents will tend to answer the open-ended question with facts and descriptive detail. You want them to respond with something that tells you about their emotional and intellectual lives. Remember when you had to write book reports in school? For most students, the first book report is simply a matter of rehashing the plot and closing with a statement that you liked the book very much.

Once you ask an open-ended question, you must

Figure 6.5 Some Questions to Help Candidates Reveal Themselves

- Tell me the duties in your last job you liked least. Most?
- We work under considerable pressure here. Have you worked under pressure in the past? How did you handle it?
- Do you prefer to work by yourself or closely with other people?
- What is your "dream job"—the perfect job for you?
- Tell me about a job-related problem you had at your last job and how you were able to solve it.
- How would you describe yourself using approximately fifty words?
- Pick some adjectives you would use to describe yourself.
- Pick some adjectives that would definitely not describe you.
- Why have you applied for this position?
- What areas of job performance are you going to need the most help with here—things like putting off work, dealing with members, job-related math, paperwork, promptness, etc.?
- What things in your life are you most proud of?
- How do you think you have grown through your work experience? What have you learned?
- Do you consider yourself methodical or instinctive? In other words, how carefully do you tend to think things through before you act?

Activity 6.1
Open, Closed, or Blended Questions?

O C B 1. Which high school did you attend?

O C B 2. Why do you enjoy working with money?

O C B 3. Have you always lived in this part of the country?

O C B 4. Do you have an account at this credit union?

O C B 5. I see your address is Whitcomb Terrace. Where in town in that?

O C B 6. Will you be driving a car to work, or using public transportation?

O C B 7. How did you enjoy your band experience in high school?

O C B 8. I see you studied French in high school. Did you find it easier than I did?

O C B 9. Are you familiar with word processing equipment?

O C B 10. Why do you say you enjoy working with people?

Answers to these questions are in appendix A at the back of this book.

THE INTERVIEW

Figure 6.6 Some Additional Interview Questions to Choose From

It is often a hard task to come up with interview questions. You will notice on the list of interview questions in figure 6.6 that the same type of question can be asked in a number of different ways. Select the approach which best matches your style and compliments the other types of questions you will be asking. A number of management related questions are also offered.

Sample Interview Questions

1. Why do you want this job?
2. What do you consider to be your greatest strength? Can you give me an example?
3. What do you consider to be your greatest weakness? How do you handle this in relation to your job responsibilities?
4. What motivates you to put forth your greatest effort?
5. What qualifies you for this job?
6. What are the most important short-term and long-term rewards you expect in your career?
7. What do you see yourself doing five years from now and what are your long-range career objectives?
8. Why should I hire you?
9. What qualifications do you have that make you think you will be successful in this job?
10. How do you determine or evaluate success?
11. What two or three accomplishments have given you the most satisfaction. Why?
12. How would your previous manager describe you?
13. What was your most significant professional achievement?
14. What was your worst professional mistake?
15. What would be your first actions once you got the job?
16. What is your ideal supervisor? What kind of work environment and management style motivates you?
17. Do you consider yourself a team player? Can you give me an example?
18. What do you know about our agency or our programs?
19. What contributions do you think you could make in this job?
20. Describe the best working relationship that should exist between a supervisor and those reporting to her.
21. How well do you handle pressure or a stressful work environment? Can you share a recent example?
22. How would you describe yourself as an employee?
23. How do you think you are perceived by your peers?
24. What are the reasons for your success in this profession?
25. What is your energy level like? Describe a typical day.
26. Why do you want to work here?
27. What kind of experience do you have for this job?
28. Are you willing to travel?
29. What did you like/dislike about your last job?
30. How do you feel about the progress in your career to date?
31. Have you done the best work you are capable of doing or have you reached your full potential in applying your skills on the job?
32. How long would it take for you to make a contribution to our company?
33. What interests you about this job?
34. What salary range are you looking for? How flexible are you on this?
35. What are you looking for in your next job?
36. What can you do for us that someone else cannot do?
37. Describe a difficult problem you have had to deal with.
38. What have you learned from the jobs you have held?
39. What would your references say?
40. What type of decisions did you make on your last job?
41. In your last job, what were some of the things you spent most of your time on, and why?

Figure 6.6 Some Additional Interview Questions to Choose From–*continued*   *page 2*

42. Do you prefer working with others or alone?
43. What kind of decisions are most difficult for you?
44. Can you explain these gaps in employment?
45. Define cooperation and teamwork.
46. Why have you changed jobs so frequently?
47. Why do you want to leave your current job?
48. What interests you least about this job?
49. What was there about your last company that you didn't particularly like or agree with?
50. What do you feel is a satisfactory attendance record? Do you feel you meet these expectations?
51. How would you describe your last company?
52. What are some of the problems you encounter in doing your job and what did you do about them?
53. What things do you find difficult to do? Why do you feel this way? How do you handle them?
54. Jobs have pluses and minuses. What were some of the minuses on your last job?
55. What kind of people do you like to work with?
56. What kind of people do you find it difficult to work with?
57. How have you successfully worked with this difficult type of person?
58. How did you get your last job?
59. How do you take direction?
60. Would you like to have your supervisor's job?
61. What do you think of your current supervisor?
62. Describe a situation where your work or an idea was criticized.
63. What have you done that shows initiative?
64. What are some of the things about which you and your supervisor disagreed?
65. In what areas do you feel your supervisor could have done a better job?
66. What are some of the job-related activities your supervisor did that you did not agree with?
67. How well do you feel your boss rated your job performance?
68. What personal characteristics are necessary for success in your field?
69. Have you ever hired or fired anyone?
70. Give an example of a time when you were able to effectively communicate with another person even though that person may have disliked you.
71. Give an example of a time when you were able to build motivation in your co-workers or those you supervised.
72. Give an example of a problem you had at work and tell me how you solved it.
73. What did you do on your last job in order to help build teamwork?
74. What are two things you wish to avoid in your next job?
75. Describe an important goal that you've set in the past, and tell me about your plans and success in reaching it.
76. What types of decisions are hard for you?
77. Give an example of a time when you had to be relatively quick in coming to a decision.
78. Describe the most significant written document/report/presentation that you had to complete.
79. Tell me some specific techniques you used on your last job in order to improve your organization and time management.
80. What is the most creative work-related project you've been involved in?
81. Tell me about a time when you had to go above and beyond the call of duty in order to get a job done.
82. What have you learned from your mistakes?
83. Describe a time on any job when you've confronted problems or stresses that tested your coping skills. What did you do?
84. Give me an example of a specific occasion when you conformed to a policy with which you didn't agree.
85. Tell me about a time when you had to delay finishing a task or speaking out because you didn't have enough information to come to a good decision.

guide the applicant into giving you the basis she has for decisions, not just the decisions themselves. When you say, "Tell me about the time you spent in the Army," you don't want a step-by-step summary of jobs and ranks. You want to know about types of jobs held, how the candidate fared away from home, how well she adapted to new and challenging environments, and so on. This nonfactual information will reveal a side of the applicant you won't see discussed on the resume.

Put another way, if you don't ask open-ended questions, there's little reason to conduct an interview. A comprehensive multiple choice test will probably serve you just as well. An interviewer who asks only closed-ended questions probably won't remain an interviewer for long.

Not all questions can be classified as either open-ended or closed-ended. Sometimes you can ask a question which, although it can technically be answered yes or no with a single phrase, actually asks for an additional

---

Let your applicant decide what his answers are in the interview. Don't lead him with your questions.

Activity 6.2
Leading or Non-Leading Questions?

L	NL	1.	What brought you to this part of the country?
L	NL	2.	If you get this position, can I assume you will be moving your personal accounts here?
L	NL	3.	You don't have any problem with overtime on Monday nights, do you?
L	NL	4.	Have you ever worked with money before?
L	NL	5.	Would you be willing to go through a telephone skills service training course?
L	NL	6.	I trust we can count on you to volunteer for our Annual Bingo Nite at the fair?
L	NL	7.	Do you have any objection to working evenings in the drive-up window?
L	NL	8.	On Fridays our tellers frequently don't get lunch until late in the day because the plant across the road has payroll on Friday morning. That won't be a problem, will it?

Answers to these questions are in appendix A at the back of this book.

response. We will call these *blended* questions. For example, if you are asked, "Did you enjoy your high school experience?" a simple yes or no response is clearly inadequate. A blended question asks for more than yes or no, but it's not as wide open as an open-ended question.

2. Don't ask leading questions. In courtroom television, we have all seen attorneys object that the other attorney was "leading the witness." We ask a leading question when we phrase it to reveal exactly what we want to hear for an answer.

Some leading questions:

- "We like our employees to get involved in community activities. You do have an interest in those sorts of things, don't you?"
- "You didn't really leave the Ephemeron Corporation because of the weather in the northwest, did you?"
- "But I suppose salary wasn't the problem there, was it?"
- "You don't mind working overtime, do you?"

Leading questions give the candidate the chance to hedge the truth and tell you what you want to hear. In a sense, they are a trap. They do you no good, and they only put the candidate in a difficult position if the truth isn't what you want to hear. Let your applicant decide what his answers are in the interview. Don't lead him with your questions.

3. You don't have to ask a question to get an answer. Experienced interviewers know they will sometimes get good information in response to a statement rather than in using a question. It seems there's something in all of us that feels challenged by a question. We get defensive and hold back a little in revealing the answer. But when we are given a statement that seems to beg a response, we are more apt to be forthcoming in our reaction. Rather than ask "Why did you leave your job at Fairway?" you might say "Your application says you left Fairway because of a personality conflict with your supervisor." Such a statement generally will draw the applicant out on the subject.

4. Ask all applicants the same basic questions before you talk about individual experiences. We all learn early on in our business development that you can't compare apples and oranges. In job interviewing, however, you need to balance your need to assess each applicant's individuality with the legally-mandated procedures of the hiring process.

Once you get past the basic format of questions, you can get personal. If someone has moved through three jobs in the last four years, some probing of stability is an obvious area of exploration. If someone has spent four years in a course of study, and then abandoned it to apply for your

THE INTERVIEW

opening, ask about it. Trying to approach a varied group of applicants with the same questions is cookie cutter interviewing and will not get you the information you want. Job interviewing simply isn't that simple.

5. Use two-part questions. You can break a complicated question into two parts to yield you the results you want. Your first question will usually be more general, and it will set up the second, more probing question. The follow-up second question forces the applicant to think on his or her feet.

As an example, you might ask, "What was your favorite subject in school?" If the applicant answers "Math and science," you might reply, "What is it in math and science that appeals to you?" Another example: "What types of accountability did you have at your job at Foremost? How often did you have to report in to your boss?" If the applicant responds by saying, "I had to submit a report to my supervisor at the end of each day," you may want to ask, "Do you think this was a proper level of accountability? Too strict or too loose?"

Activity 6.3

Practicing Your Probes

For each of the following questions (and unsatisfactory answers), write down a follow-up question to get at the information you need.

1. • "I see you spent a year and a half at Pine Bluff Community College. How did you like it?"
   • "I would just as soon not talk about that."

   Probe: _____

2. • "I see there is nothing in your resume for the years 1987 and 1988. What were you doing then?"
   • "Nothing much, really. Hanging around."

   Probe: _____

3. • "I see from your employment history you were in the accounts payable department at the Wimpett Corporation. What did you like and not like about the job?"
   • "Do you really have to know? I had some bad times there I would rather not talk about."

   Probe: _____

4. • "Promptness is very important to us. Has that been a problem for you at previous jobs?"
   • "Well, not really. I mean things eventually worked out, anyway."

   Probe: _____

Suggested answers can be found in appendix A at the back of this book.

6. Don't ask complex questions. You face several dangers in asking multi-part or highly structured questions. First, the candidate may simply not follow you and you will have to repeat or simplify your request for information. Second, the candidate may choose to address the simplest portion of the question and leave unanswered the more difficult or more probing part. Asking complex questions in the pressure cooker atmosphere of a job interview is not efficient. The candidate, especially at the start of the interview, may be tense and somewhat impaired by nervousness. Simple questions, skillfully asked, can tell you everything you want to know about a candidate.

7. Probe when you have to, but softly. Inevitably, you're going to have to ask some questions that may cause discomfort. Perhaps the applicant was fired from a recent job. Or a reference was half-hearted at best. Or you ask about a previous job and get an answer that doesn't say anything. If you tell yourself, the applicant doesn't want to talk about it, you are not doing your job. If you felt the question was important enough to ask, it should be important enough to be answered.

There's nothing wrong with saying, "Could you tell me a little more about what you mean by a personality conflict with Rachel Winston? You will be dealing with personalities here as well, and I want to understand what you feel happened with Rachel." While you should be cordial and non-confrontational, any old answer won't do. If the question is ducked, be sensitive but persistent.

Don't, however, let your probes make the interview turn unpleasant. Soften your probing questions. Let the applicant know why you need to know what you're asking. Help the applicant find a comfortable way to answer you. Explain why the information is important. Underscore the confidentiality of the interview itself. Perhaps you have been a little cold and overprofessional; try a little warmth.

Your job is to get answers, not just to ask questions. Don't accept nonanswers. Later, you will wind up looking at your notes and seeing you learned next to nothing in the interview.

If you spot a red flag in an answer or nonanswer, you have a duty to resolve it. If you don't, you're going to decide not to hire this person based on what you *don't* know. If you're uncomfortable enough with a topic the candidate is ducking, tell the candidate how you feel.

"Michael, I need you to give me more detail about what happened in this job you didn't mention in your resume or job application. I don't understand the connection between these events. Help me understand."

Figure 6.7 Asking Questions During the Interview

1. Ask open-ended questions.
2. Don't ask leading questions.
3. You don't have to ask a question to get an answer.
4. Ask all applicants the same basic questions before you talk about individual experiences.
5. Use two-part questions.
6. Don't ask complex questions.
7. Probe when you have to, but softly.

Controlling the Interview

1. Stay in charge of the interview. You're the one responsible for getting the information you need from the interview for making the hiring decision. If you let a well-prepared candidate spend your time talking about what he wants to talk about, you haven't done your job. Keep focused on the information you need. Keep your attention on developing an understanding of how well this person would fit into the position you're trying to fill. Applicants generally feel on the defensive in the interview situation. They know what they *don't* want to talk about. And they will try hard to keep conversation restricted to their personal comfort areas. You must resist the temptation to digress in "happy talk." Treat the interview as a business meeting, because that's exactly what it is.

   When inexperienced interviewers sense their control of the interview slipping away, they often feel they can regain mastery by simply talking more. This is the wrong approach. Exert control again with simple, direct phrases, such as: "We've drifted a bit here. Let's go back to your record at Mountain States College" or "Your supervisor sounds like a character. Time is starting to catch up on us here. Tell me about your next job, at the power company in Akron." A gentle nudge should do the job.

2. Keep the interview on course. In the overview statement, you told the applicant the plan you had for the interview's course. If you stray from this—or it becomes evident to the applicant that there is, in fact, no plan—you are in trouble. You will end up with blank spaces where you need information. And you won't be giving the applicant a fair shot at the job. Stay with your overview plan: employment, education, gaps, applicant questions. Don't leave the employment section of the interview until you have satisfied your questions in that area. Don't move back and forth across subject matters; this is inefficient and leads to a rambling, often incoherent chat. Refer frequently to your talk/listening points to track your progress. And keep an eye on the clock.

   There was a trend a few years back in interviewing toward what became known as the *free-form interview.* The idea was that a loose conversation between interviewer and applicant would reveal whether there was a good match between the two and, therefore, between the candidate and the job. In fact, this technique was normally an excuse for an unprepared interviewer. You hire an employee based on a free-wheeling conversation.

It's always best to conduct a structured interview, with significant planning done before the candidate even enters the room. Your results will be better. And you won't find yourself in the awkward position of looking at a gap in your understanding of the candidate's background. There's no easy way to fill that gap except by an embarrassing call to the applicant. The structured interview also helps ensure that, if your hiring decisions are ever challenged in court, you will be able to show the sound basis for your judgment.

An outline of your interview process becomes extremely valuable in a number of situations. For example, when you are faced with multiple interviews in a short period of time. It is very easy to lose your focus and begin asking yourself, "Now where am I, what do I still need to cover?" It is also a useful tool to help manage your time and keep your interview on schedule. If you have a number of interviews scheduled over one or two weeks, it helps you to get organized and quickly familiar with the process once again. Figure

6.8 includes a sample interview format.

You should also pass up what's termed the stress interview. Here, the interviewer deliberately puts the candidate through anxiety-producing moments in the interview to determine how well she holds up to stress. The interviewer might say to a B.A. in history that they have never had any luck hiring a liberal arts major at this credit union. Or an interviewer might sketch out a fictional situation at the credit union, express grave concern, and ask the applicant how she might solve it.

3. Don't be gullible. Interview manuals instruct candidates to make every effort to establish a personal bond with you. After all, they argue, it's easier to turn down someone you don't know for a job than someone you know. If a candidate comments on a family picture you have on the desk and says she has a daughter the same age as yours, react

Figure 6.8 The Structured Interview

I.	PLAN THE INTERVIEW
II.	SCHEDULE & BEGIN THE INTERVIEW
III.	ORIENT APPLICANT TO THE INTERVIEW
IV.	DESCRIBE THE POSITION
V.	INITIATE QUESTIONS & LISTEN
VI.	CONCLUDE THE INTERVIEW
VII.	REVIEW THE INTERVIEW

If a candidate comments on a family picture you have on the desk and says she has a daughter the same age as yours, react politely. But put your guard up.

politely. But put your guard up. You are interviewing someone who is out to "win your heart." There is a shelf full of "how to get hired" books out there that coach applicants to make such compliments to the interviewer.

You may find candidates speaking about the difficulties of your job in interviewing candidates, about your abilities in holding such a lofty position in the credit union, about how desperately they need the job, about how they are about to turn around their life now and all they need is a break, and so on.

Your responsibility is to make an objective appraisal of the candidate. Don't be distracted by pulls at the heartstrings or your ego, no matter how sincere they may appear. Think of the situation you are in when you go to buy a car. You gather information. You take what the salesperson says respectfully, but with a grain of salt. You are well aware that

his job is to sell a car, not to make your life happier.

In your interviewing role, you should be sincere and friendly. But you should also put on your "game face," a serious turn of mind that analyzes skeptically all of the information you are receiving. Don't let any candidate sweet-talk you into awarding a job. Be sensitive to these tactics. If they become blatant, refocus the applicant to concentrate on the substance of the interview.

4. Good candidates are bought, not sold. Every candidate comes to the interview with a single goal in mind: sell myself so they offer me the job. Your job is to avoid the sell and, instead, gather the kind of information you need to make the hiring decision that's best for the credit union.

As you will see later in the decision-making portion of the hiring process, you are going to make this decision by looking at the information you received as objectively as possible. Don't hire someone on charm, or a lively sense of humor, or a basically irresistible personality. We have all met these golden people that light up a room when they walk in. The question you must answer is how good an employee they will make for your credit union.

Remember, a super-polished applicant may mean you are simply talking with someone who's gone through all the interview books. This interview preparation industry is a big business in

Figure 6.9 Controlling the Interview

1. Stay in charge of the interview.
2. Keep the interview on course.
3. Don't be gullible.
4. Good candidates are bought, not sold.

America, especially at times when the job market tightens up. Don't buy the polish, buy the applicant. Hire on qualifications.

Testing and Assessment Techniques

Testing and assessment seems to be falling out of favor in the labor market the last few years. There are probably several reasons for this.

- The job market in some categories is tighter than it was and employers are actively looking for people to hire, not for people to exclude.
- Testing has gotten a bad name in some ways in preselecting candidates with test-taker mentalities. Some people do well on tests, even though they are no more qualified than others. Successful test taking is simply a knack those candidates are fortunate enough to have.
- Equal employment laws have been applied to testing situations and there are some specific standards these tests must meet. Many professionals involved in hiring steer clear of all pre-employment tests other than those that test a simple skill like typing, spelling, reading, or math skills.
- Test results don't always correlate to performance in the workplace.

There are times when tests make sense and have a clear value.

- You can devise a test which clearly examines the applicant's skills for the job: typing tests for secretaries, physical endurance tests for firefighters, math tests for financial personnel.
- They provide simply one more part of a full evaluation.

Few credit unions perform testing of job applicants at the entry level beyond a straightforward mathematical aptitude test and/or a typing test. You can find fundamental typing and math tests at most libraries, at large bookstores, or through a phone call to a local employment or temporary agency.

The testing marketplace is filled with tests that make claims of relevance to job performance. Of course, these may have nothing to do with the position for which you are hiring. Some of these tests include:

- Honesty tests are written tests that reveal a candidate's propensity to dishonesty.
- Sales aptitude tests reveal the selling skills possessed by the applicant. This can lead to increased cross-sales success, especially in jobs that involve considerable public contact.
- Personality tests seek to reveal the core personality of candidates, providing management with an inside look at the person they are considering hiring.
- Proponents say handwriting analysis (or graphoanalysis) provides an inexpensive way to screen out high-risk persons.

Figure 6.10 Sometimes Aptitude is Not What You Think

During World War II, when great numbers of trained technicians were in demand, it was assumed that those who had mechanical aptitude would make good airplane mechanics. A careful analysis of this assumption proved otherwise. It turned out that a good shoe clerk in civilian life would make a better mechanic for military purposes than someone who had fixed cars most of his life. The critical trait was not mechanical aptitude, but the ability of the trainee to follow instructions. The Army then worked out its instruction manuals so meticulously that the best recruit turned out to be a mildly obsessional person who could read and follow instructions. The last thing they wanted was someone with his own ideas on how to fix equipment.

Edward T. Hall, *The Silent Language*, 1959

- Dependability tests measure an applicant's attitudes, practices, and values that are job-related. It attempts to predict future success in the job.

The testing industry has responded to the attacks on its validity by developing a series of new tests, and checking these new instruments extensively. Unfortunately, individual states are not in agreement on which tests have any validity, resulting in an extremely clouded national picture.

Unless you can be convinced by your testing materials supplier that the test results will stand up in court, you probably should forego pre-employment testing.

Human resources journals will carry advertisements from nationally-known test developers. Review their literature and make your own decision. Always keep in mind that you may one day be asked, while on the witness stand, "How do you know the results of this test truly predict better job performance in the position for which you used this test?"

Summary

Extend every effort to make your candidate comfortable in the interview. An uncomfortable candidate is difficult to judge. Use your questioning skills to draw from the candidate the information not covered in the resume or application. Have the candidate answer your questions, both the ones you ask of all candidates, and those specific to the applicant in question. Encourage the applicant to talk about herself by the use of open-ended questions.

Make sure you stay on track with your interview outline. Use notes to record your impressions of the interview and the specific answers of the candidate. Some credit unions utilize standardized tests to screen candidates for particular skills or character traits. Get a legal opinion before considering such testing.

Chapter Seven: Selecting Your Candidate

What's going to sell you on a candidate? In addition to job qualifications, you're going to want to have some sense that the candidate has presented herself fairly—that the applicant's been internally consistent in telling his or her story—and that you feel the applicant would make a workable addition to your workforce.

Here's where you take out your evaluation grid (see chapter 3) and enter a rating based on the interview with each candidate. By now you have been through all the steps with each candidate and scored each individual in every category. A decision should start to emerge from your analysis.

Be objective. Separate the rush of the hiring process and getting a neat person from a business-like evaluation where you match the applicant's skills with the requirements of the particular position. Don't hire based on charm. There may be such a thing as love at first sight, but we all know there's also false love at first sight. Question your analysis of candidates. How would you respond if your superior asked, "In a nutshell, why do you think this is the best person for us?"

Don't consider the applicants solely in relation to one another. You are not involved in a rating game. The question is how well the candidates match the job qualifications you have outlined. All applicants may match the

Objectives

> **Upon completion of this chapter, you will be able to:**
>
> 1. **Select the winning candidate on the basis of all that's gone before, and according to the job-related criteria previously established.**
>
> 2. **Use an evaluation grid to make the most objective determination possible.**

qualifications, or none may. If all do, then which applicants seem strongest in those areas of the job qualifications you have ranked as most important?

Matching Skills with Job Requirements

Workplace research has demonstrated that in simple jobs, turnover is greatest among those that are over-qualified; in the more challenging jobs, turnover is greatest among those that are under-qualified. This should serve as a cautionary note against hiring the over-qualified. They will get bored and will never grow content in a job that doesn't tax their abilities. In the same vein, there's no wisdom in hiring someone with good people skills and good work habits and putting that person in charge of a complicated computer operation. Don't underwhelm or overwhelm your candidates. You will both lose.

Every person who's ever screened people to fill a job opening knows the feeling of looking at a stack of resumes and cover letters. We look for reasons to rule people out. We insist on an arbitrary level of education or training as a device for weeding out some of the applicants. Since education and experience are somewhat quantifiable (we can attach numbers to them), they give us a more comfortable way to rank our fellow human beings.

In training camp for rookies, before they are signed for professional football teams, most halfbacks run sprints against a stopwatch. If they can't beat a particular speed standard, they are out of the running for a professional career. We like to judge by numbers because they make it easier on us. But the fact remains that this simplicity causes the professional sports ranks, not to mention credit unions, to lose out on some desirable and talented people.

In hiring and recruiting circles, there's a theory of hiring called self-selection. Given relatively full information about the work involved in a job, most people who aren't suited for the job won't apply for it. In other words, people tend to have a pretty clear sense of their own strengths and weaknesses. Show them the job, and those most fit for it will apply. While there's some truth to this framework, it breaks down when the potential applicants are under extreme pressure. There may be times in most of our lives when it boils down to needing a job, *any* job.

Never underestimate the importance of chances for advancement to job applicants. Job advancement means more money and recognition, and there's not one of us immune to the appeal of that. Even people who are only planning on keeping the job for a year or two can still be drawn by an appeal to their basic desire for more money and recognition.

One of the sobering facts about employee hiring is that most of the mismatches—where an employee and his or her job don't work out together—are the result of characteristics that should have been evident in the initial hiring interview.

Fitting the Personality into the Existing Work Environment

Professional personnel managers remind us not to make the mistake of treating every job as if it's a career. While we ought to make sure that each employee understands the promotion path from his or her current position, we don't want to make the mistake of assuming that each of our employees must possess the qualities on which to build a career with the credit union. Promotability is not important in all jobs. Recall the "Peter Principle," the rage of management consulting a few years back. The Peter Principle says we are all eventually promoted to the level of our own incompetence. A very good teller is promoted to teller supervisor. She doesn't do well there because the talents that made her a good teller aren't those needed by a good supervisor. Or perhaps she received inadequate supervisory training to prepare for the new role.

In all the advertisements for mutual funds we see in the financial magazines, we see the disclaimer that the quoted results are historical and don't necessarily mean that the fund will perform in a similar manner in the future. In the same way, a resume and job application show us the past of a person, and some of the skills this person has accumulated during that past. Just how well we can see into this person's future with our credit union is problematical. On the other hand, what better ways are there to judge the prospects of future success?

Managers constantly face the dilemma of picking people whose personality traits place them somewhere along the spectrum of dependability and initiative. A case could be argued that a credit union is a place that's perhaps better suited to dependable rather than highly initiative-driven individuals. Top management

Figure 7.1 Vigor in Dissent: The Independent Employee

Vigor in dissent is the hallmark of a dedicated employee; its presence indicates a self-confident, intelligent management. Vigor in acceptance is a recognition, on the part of the employee, that the organization must require acceptance. The absence of either is fatal.

Milton W Mandell, *The Selection Process*

may be an exception to this opinion. If you choose a dependable person, are you willing to live with the lack of initiative? If you choose a person with initiative, are you willing to put up with occasional bouts of trouble stemming from that initiative?

Summary

Your decision must come from your best efforts to match the skills of the candidate with the skills demanded by the job as outlined in the job description. Ask yourself just what sort of person will do best in this job as you have defined it. Again, you must be as objective as possible. Your evaluation grid will enable you to review and rate the candidates.

Chapter Eight: Delivering the News

Courtesy is reason enough to make your decision promptly. Depending on the number and timing of interviews, you should make no candidate wait more than a week for the decision.

How to Say No to the Unsuccessful Candidate

The best way to notify unsuccessful candidates for the position is a letter. This avoids the discomfort of a phone call and provides them written notification of how their application turned out. Avoid writing a cold and detached letter. Remember, this applicant has gone to considerable trouble applying for your job—sending in a resume, filling out an application, possibly taking tests, and so on. And don't forget this candidate has friends and family that probably are aware she has applied to your credit union. If the candidate feels ill-treated through a callous "no thanks" letter, you may damage your reputation in the community. Deliver any bad news gently.

Out of courtesy to the top contenders you interviewed, and possibly called back for a second interview, give your decision in a phone call. Don't take the easy way out with a letter. Be graceful and honest in telling them the bad news.

Objectives

Upon completion of this chapter, you will be able to:

1. **Notify the winning candidate promptly and formally about his or her selection, and make the actual job offer.**

2. **Develop a letter giving the winning candidate all necessary information to start work.**

3. **Notify the candidates that were not selected with sensitivity.**

Out of courtesy to the top contenders you interviewed, and possibly called back for a second interview, give your decision in a phone call.

Figure 8.1 Sample Letter to an Interviewed Candidate Not Selected

Dear Ms. Phillips:

I would like to thank you for your time spent applying and interviewing for our position of assistant bookkeeper. We have offered the position to another candidate and that person has accepted. We feel we have selected the applicant that best matched the position.

I know this isn't the outcome you wanted. We were impressed by the skills you showed in your interview and supporting documents.

With your strong background and talents, I am confident you will be able to find yourself in desirable employment shortly.

Thank you for thinking of us here at the Anytown Credit Union. I enjoyed meeting you.

Figure 8.2 Additional Letter for a Candidate Not Selected

October 17, 1991

Jane Smith
4381 Clearing Road
Mt. Pleasant, WI

Dear Jane:
Thank you for taking the time to interview with us for the position of

_____.

As you can appreciate, we had a considerable number of applicants for the position available. We spoke with several qualified candidates, and the final selection was difficult. We have, however, made our final selection in favor of another applicant.

The resume that you submitted will be kept on file for one year. Again, thank you for your interest in employment with CUNA & Affiliates.

Sincerely,

John Mosely
Human Resources

/clk

Figure 8.3 A Sample Job Offer Letter

Dear Ms. Phillips:
This letter is to confirm our conversation of last Friday. After reviewing all applicants for the position of Assistant Bookkeeper, I would like to offer you the job.

The salary rate for the position is $5.95 per hour. The work hours are 8:30 a.m. to 5:30 p.m. Monday through Friday. You will be working at our Greenville Branch. Your supervisor will be Virginia Bresnahan. As we discussed on the phone, we are expecting you to start work on Monday, November 3. At that time, Virginia will brief you more fully on your job responsibilities, set you up with the personnel department for a review of your benefits, and make arrangements to get you into training.

I am happy to have you as a member of Anytown Credit Union. If you have any questions before your start date, please feel free to call me. We very much look forward to having you as a member of our team.

How to Say Yes to the Successful Candidate

Giving the news to the successful candidate is much more pleasant. No interviewer needs to be prodded to make that phone call.

Generally, the first notice to the successful candidate is given over the phone, just as soon as you have made the decision. Tell the applicant that he or she has the job, restate the title of the position, and the salary rate. Be careful to make no statement which might suggest any sort of long-term employment contract. Make the job offer clear and unambiguous, including what you would like as a starting date. Ask the applicant if he would like to give you the okay now. If he needs to think about it, fine. But tell the applicant you will need a call within a specified period of time—normally the end of the next working day.

Once your phone offer is accepted, send a letter restating the details of the job offer. Putting the offer in writing will avoid any unpleasant misunderstandings later on.

Once your hiring decision is made, and your candidate accepts, send out letters to the unsuccessful candidates, both those you have interviewed and those you haven't.

Summary

Once you make your decision, notify the winning candidate promptly with a phone call *and* follow-up in writing. Set a deadline for the applicant's decision on accepting the position. Once an applicant accepts the job, notify the other candidates of your decision. Be certain your new employee has all the information necessary to begin work.

Figure 8.4 Additional Job Offer Letter

November 25, 1991

Corine Gregory
5831 Atwood Blvd.
Maine, GA 87353

Dear Ms. Gregory:
WELCOME TO CUNA & AFFILIATES! We are pleased to confirm our offer of employment as Program Assistant which commences on December 1, 1991. Your normal work hours will be 8:00 a.m. to 4:00 p.m. with a starting salary of $6.05 per hour.

Enclosed are some pre-employment forms and brochures highlighting health benefits, along with the premium costs, offered to employees of CUNA & Affiliates. Please review and complete the material *prior* to your orientation on December 1. Attached is a checklist to guide you in completing these forms.

Please arrive on Monday December 1, for orientation at 8:00 a.m. and feel free to park in the visitors parking area. A representative from Human Resources will then greet you and other new employees in the lobby area. You will start the day with an informational benefits overview where you will receive more detailed explanations.

Due to the fact that the Immigration Reform Act requires all employers to hire only U.S. citizens or aliens authorized lawfully to work in the United States, please bring documentation to prove your identity. See documentation lists in Section 2 of "Employment Eligibility Verification" form. We require either one document from List A or one document from List B *and* one document from List C.

After the informational benefits overview, your supervisor, Greg Van Etten, will meet with you and share pertinent information regarding your work responsibilities at CUNA & Affiliates.

We look forward to having you with us. If you have any questions, please don't hesitate to call me at (608)231-4325.

Sincerely,

Sandra Quame
Human Resources

cc: Personnel file
Enclosure

Chapter Nine: Summary

The first few employment interviews most managers conduct are somewhat uneasy experiences. There's something in us that's uncomfortable sitting in judgment on others. Despite the fact that we do these interviews because our credit union feels we are qualified to do the job, we still don't look forward to it.

This manual has covered a lot of ground, from personality types to legal guidelines, from interview tips to reference-checking guidelines, from body language to plain language. At this point, you should be considerably more capable of conducting a solid, professional job interview. And you should be more sensitive to some of the fine points. You should go back to your interviewing work with two main parting thoughts.

First of all, good hiring demands good preparation. There's no substitute for basic groundwork. Regardless of your wonderful insight into human nature or your cleverness in phrasing questions, you won't consistently hire good people without entering into the hiring process primed to land a first-class employee.

This manual has shown you these steps.
- Understanding the legal context of the hiring process
- Knowing the benefits package offered by your credit union

Objectives

Upon completion of this chapter, you will be able to:

1. **Do an excellent job of preparing yourself for the hiring process.**

2. **Maintain the "human touch" in all personnel-related actions.**

- Conducting an exit interview of the departing employee
- Reviewing the job and job description for which you are hiring (revising what you must)
- Recruiting applicants intelligently

The quality of motivation that appears in a man's work is not so much instilled in him by managerial practices as it is elicited from him by his job.

Saul W. Gellerman, Management by Motivation

- Studying resumes and applications thoroughly and selecting the best people to interview
- Conducting a comprehensive and professional interview
- Making a solid decision and making it promptly

If you approach your hiring as a normal part of your business operations, as opposed to a periodic space-filling procedure, you

SUMMARY

will get better results. Make a hiring procedures checklist. Use it yourself, and pass it around to other managers for their counsel. This will save you time in subsequent hiring.

Successful managers also critique their own hiring performance. How well did the search for candidates go? Did the job description reflect the actual job duties and skills required? Were the interviews concise and productive? As you go through more and more hiring situations, you will refine both your people skills and your standardized hiring procedures. Each new employee will come on board a little easier than the last.

The second major point you should bear in mind is to keep

Activity 9.1
Create your own hiring procedures checklist.

• Review all job descriptions at least annually.

• In assessing existing employees, make notes on those who might not remain with the credit union.

_____

_____

_____

_____

_____

• Evaluate strategic plans (and revisions) for possible personnel impacts.

_____

_____

_____

_____

• List newspapers (or other media) in which you should run recruitment ads.

_____

_____

_____

_____

• Develop a relationship (if relevant) with a local employment or temporary agency for fill-in assistance between regular employees. The same applies to a testing service.

_____

_____

_____

_____

the human *touch* in everything you do about hiring. It takes a little life experience to be able to hire well. Some people are naturally good judges of character, and some aren't. You have to try to balance a healthy skepticism with a frank openness.

Don't ever forget that in answering each of your questions, the candidate is trying to balance the truth with what he thinks you *want* to hear. Very few candidates will actually lie in an interview, but they may go out of their way to appear better than they are. It's your job to try to *objectify* the hiring process—to brush away the fog to judge the real person.

Holding the power of hiring or not hiring is an influential position. Make every effort to use it both wisely and sensitively, to obtain the most qualified employees you can. Choosing from among a group of candidates can test your powers of discernment. It can be a complicated process, taking place as it does in an intimidating legal climate. And it can be personally exhausting as well. But hiring the right people can fire up your credit union with excitement and make all your efforts worthwhile.

Appendix A: Answers to Activities

The answers to many of these activities simply aren't right or wrong. Some depend on your local area, others on your particular personality. Treat answers provided here as a guide, not as the sole acceptable responses.

Chapter One

Answers to Activity 1.3

Religious leader: sincere, charitable, sympathetic, unselfish

Judge: objective, studious, patient, humane, wise

Plumber: physically handy, resourceful, strong, hard-working

Accountant: good at numbers, honest, objective, law-abiding, scrupulous

Professional marathon runner: strong, fit, disciplined, stoic

Dairy farmer: diligent, hard-working, early riser

Hunting guide: self-reliant, resourceful, experienced, strong

Advertising executive: creative, smart, business-minded, quick study

Special education teacher: empathetic, patient, unselfish

Credit union teller: detailed, personable, enthusiastic, responsible

Loan officer: perceptive, detailed, objective

Chapter Two

Answers to Activity 2.1

Teller Position Ad

Financial institution seeks mid-level teller. Should have 2 years experience. Bondable. 35–40 hours weekly; some weekend hours. Skill with money handling important. Good benefits and competitive salary. We are an equal opportunity employer. Respond to...

Bookkeeper Position Ad

Financial institution seeks bookkeeper. Must be familiar with standard mini computer financial tracking programs. Should have 3–5 years experience. Bondable. 40 hours weekly. Reliability and attention to detail very important.

Position may lead to major branch bookkeeping responsibility. Good benefits and competitive salary. We are an equal opportunity employer. Respond to…

New Accounts Person Ad

People-oriented person to handle walk-in and referral work on new accountholders. Will need to become familiar with institutional operation quickly, since interaction with other departments is important. Must follow detailed instructions and work with people on filling out detailed forms. Good benefits and competitive salary. We are an equal opportunity employer. Respond to…

Chapter Three

Answers to Activity 3.1
(Answers will vary, yours may be similar to the ones below.)

1. What qualifies you for this job?
2. What kind of experiences do you have for this job?
3. How well do you handle pressure as a stressful work environment? Can you share a recent example?
4. Do you prefer working with others or alone?
5. Define cooperation and teamwork.
6. Give me an example of a problem you had at work and tell me how you solved it.

Chapter Five

Answers to Activity 5.1

1. D	7. D	13. N	19. D
2. D	8. S	14. D	20. S
3. D	9. D	15. D	21. D
4. D	10. N	16. D	22. D
5. D	11. S	17. D	23. D
6. N	12. D	18. D	

Chapter Six

Answers to Activity 6.1

1. C	6. C
2. O	7. D
3. B	8. B
4. C	9. C
5. B	10. O

Answers to Activity 6.2

1.	NL	5.	NL
2.	L	6.	L
3.	L	7.	NL
4.	NL	8.	L

Answers to Activity 6.3

1. I don't want to pry, but your education's an important part of your qualifying for this position. How can we talk about it?
2. Can you be more specific? Were you working or in school?
3. I don't need the details. Just give me some general idea. I don't want you to be uncomfortable, but I really need to know.
4. Were there promptness problems? Surely you can understand I have to know about your work habits. I would rather hear about them from you.

Appendix B: Test Questions

Answers to these test questions are to be marked on the scannable answer sheet provided. Please do not mark answers in the book or return the pages included in Appendix B to be graded. Photocopies of test questions and answers will not be accepted. Original scannable answer sheets are to be returned to CUNA in the envelope provided.

You may be provided with a test that includes both questions and an area for placing answers. These tests are manually graded by league staff. The questions asked on manual tests are the same as the ones listed in Appendix B. Use either list of questions when completing the answer area on your test. Photocopies of manual tests will not be accepted. Original test answer sheets for manual tests are to be returned to your league education department.

1. Generally, you will need to consult with which of the following on matters of hiring and anti-discrimination legislation?
   a. city social services
   b. Mayor's office
   c. your corporate attorney
   d. Federal Housing and Urban Development office

2. Credit union members interact regularly most often with your institution's
   a. officers.
   b. front-line workers.
   c. security people.
   d. loan officers.

3. If you expect to do a good job of hiring, you need to plan to set aside the equivalent of how much time?
   a. two days
   b. one day
   c. four hours
   d. one week

4. The first part of the hiring process is to
   a. set a salary level.
   b. establish staffing requirements.
   c. conduct an exit interview.
   d. check references.

5. One shortcoming of the exit interview is that
   a. people don't always know why they're leaving.
   b. people may not want to take part in it.
   c. you will get nothing but negative information.
   d. inside politics may become involved.

6. In some instances, the exit interview
   a. may take place after the employee is working at her new job.
   b. should be done over the telephone.
   c. must be conducted in front of a witness.
   d. should be conducted by someone other than the immediate supervisor.

7. Reevaluating a job description is sometimes referred to as
   a. job analysis.
   b. job enrichment.
   c. personnel matrix development.
   d. positional advantage.

8. In reviewing job descriptions, you should
   a. write them as if they will last for five years.
   b. learn all the details that make up the job.
   c. compare your description with national norms.
   d. submit them to the local EEOC office for approval.

9. One component not included in job description is (are)
   a. equipment which must be operated.
   b. a supervisory chain of command.
   c. a performance standard.
   d. desired personality traits.

10. It's important that you check your job description for
    a. gender-neutral language.
    b. applicability to your credit union's strategic plan.
    c. compliance with FICA requirements.
    d. simplicity.

11. In terms of salary levels, workers are generally more concerned about
    a. being able to save for retirement.
    b. insurance coverages available and exclusions included.
    c. their pay in relation to the pay of others.
    d. the chance for getting onto the management track.

12. Which of the following is *not* a component of the total compensation package?
    a. base salary
    b. value of insurance premiums paid by the credit union
    c. other benefits (daycare, healthclub membership, etc.)
    d. credit union contribution to unemployment compensation fund

13. Perhaps the best way to demonstrate to employees their total compensation package is to
    a. create a detailed visual.
    b. have your human resources person prepare a briefing.
    c. have your insurance supplier detail the coverages available.
    d. have a senior employee explain the benefits package.

14. One source of worker referrals that's often ignored is (are)
    a. other credit unions.
    b. the local office of the Job Service.
    c. agencies specializing in financial services.
    d. job fairs.

15. In these times, employees generally view the benefits package
    a. about the same as in the past.
    b. as having more value than in the past.
    c. as having less value than in the past.
    d. as relatively unimportant.

16. You should use a blind box in recruiting ads if you
    a. want the name of your credit union advertised.
    b. don't want to have to respond to all applicants.
    c. want to draw the greatest number of responses.
    d. want to avoid excessive phone calls.

17. The services of an employment agency
    a. are covered by the hired employee.
    b. guarantee the quality of hired employees.
    c. generally run between 15 and 25 percent of annual salary.
    d. are offered only on a long-term contract.

18. If you want to hire a new employee while spending the least recruitment money, you should
    a. use the local Job Service office.
    b. look into radio advertising packages for off-peak spots.
    c. speak to television stations about PSAs (public service announcements).
    d. negotiate an attractive rate with a temporary agency.

19. Job benefits generally add what percentage to the base salary?
    a. 15%
    b. 22.5%
    c. 30%
    d. 45%

20. One advantage of in-house referrals of new employees is
    a. that the applicants are more qualified.
    b. that it can be much quicker.
    c. that it enables you to avoid hiring people with credit problems.
    d. that it lets you avoid potential discrimination issues.

21. One disadvantage of in-house referrals of new employees is
    a. that friends of current employees may not get along with each other once working together.
    b. that it can prove more costly.
    c. that it restricts your labor pool.
    d. the possible disappointment if the referred applicant isn't selected.

22. Hiring a temporary for a full-time position will normally cost you
    a. nothing.
    b. $500, on the national average.
    c. 10–15 percent of the starting salary.
    d. nothing. It is against the law to hire away a temporary worker.

23. One advantage of filling a job opening with a current employee is it
    a. gives others in the organization the chance to advance as well.
    b. maximizes the training investment you have already made.
    c. avoids any discrimination issues.
    d. will generally save on salary expenditures.

24. One disadvantage of filling a job opening with a current employee is that
    a. the advanced employee may become too self-important.
    b. your salary scale will eventually creep upward.
    c. movement from one supervisor to another may cause hard feelings.
    d. you still have an opening to fill.

25. If a resume strikes you as being quite vague in terms of previous job experience,
    a. make a point of asking questions in the interview.
    b. call the references immediately.
    c. call the applicant and get an explanation over the phone.
    d. eliminate the applicant from consideration.

26. A good general policy for handling supplied references is to
    a. ignore them.
    b. call them after the interview.
    c. call them before the interview.
    d. write to them after the interview.

27. If you see frequent job changes on a job application or resume,
    a. eliminate the candidate from consideration.
    b. look for a pattern of upward movement.
    c. consider the value of the candidate's education.
    d. call the two most recent employers.

28. Establishing a base-level educational requirement for a job
    a. is customary and should probably be continued.
    b. is expected by your members.
    c. must match the genuine, provable job requirements
       as spelled out in the job description.
    d. will likely lead to less turnover in your credit union.

29. The use of an evaluation grid
    a. will enable you to objectify the hiring decision.
    b. applies only to management hires.
    c. will enable you to utilize your computer capabilities.
    d. requires personnel department supervision.

30. Asking a candidate about drug usage is
    a. expected in the financial services field.
    b. approved under the Federal Drug Act.
    c. illegal.
    d. required to keep you from potential liability suits.

31. A standardized interview outline
    a. will simplify and standardize your interviewing.
    b. will probably be found discriminatory in any court
       proceedings.
    c. is a relic of the early days of personnel practices.
    d. will lead to interviews that don't reveal the true candidate.

32. You can legally ask questions of an applicant regarding
    a. marital status, if relevant to the job position.
    b. number of children, to help you plan daycare needs.
    c. drug usage, if within last twelve months.
    d. criminal convictions, if related to financial crimes.

33. Federal laws regarding discrimination in hiring
    a. are often affected by state and local laws.
    b. have not changed significantly since 1973.
    c. can be waived, depending on local population.
    d. are generally not enforced except for flagrant violations.

34. Which of the following questions can you legally ask in an interview or on an application?
    a. Are you planning to work after the birth of your child?
    b. Can you handle the math requirements of a teller position?
    c. Have you ever been arrested for shoplifting?
    d. Have you been married before?

35. Which of the following questions can you legally ask in an interview or on an application?
    a. Have your wages ever been garnished?
    b. Are you a citizen of the United States?
    c. May I call your last two employers for a reference?
    d. What color are your eyes?

36. An interview overview statement allows you to
    a. establish the framework the interview will follow.
    b. keep the applicant from taking control of the interview.
    c. wrap up the interview and move on to the next applicant.
    d. outline your concerns about the applicant's references.

37. In an employment interview, the applicant should
    a. be encouraged to ask his or her questions at the opening.
    b. not be allowed to rebut negative information.
    c. know by the end of the interview whether he has the job.
    d. speak 80 percent of the time.

38. The notes you take in the employment interview
    a. may form the basis of a legal defense if the hiring decision is challenged.
    b. should not be noticed by the applicant.
    c. should be supported by tape recording.
    d. should be destroyed immediately after the hiring decision.

39. The main purpose of open-ended questions is to
    a. avoid legally dangerous areas.
    b. avoid the strictness of a question and answer interview.
    c. let the applicant tell you about job experience.
    d. give you a sense of the candidate's true self.

40. In general, honesty tests
    a. will reveal a person's true honesty.
    b. can let applicant's know how you feel about integrity.
    c. should be carefully checked with your legal advisors.
    d. are mandatory for workers in financial fields.

Evaluation Questions

Please complete these evaluation questions after you have taken this test. Mark appropriate answers on the scannable answer sheet under numbers 41 through 44. You may choose more than one answer for numbers 43 and 44.

41. I am taking this module through
    a. Correspondence
    b. Chapter/credit union study group
    c. League-sponsored conference/workshop

42. Overall I feel this module was
    a. Excellent
    b. Good
    c. Fair
    d. Poor

43. This module/book was
    a. Practical
    b. Irrelevant
    c. Interesting
    d. Boring

44. The Competency test was
    a. Fair
    b. Tricky
    c. Clear
    d. Vague

Management Enrichment Training Program

Participant Evaluation Sheet

Module Title _____

Credit Union or League Name _____ Date _____

Please rate this program by indicating your response using the scale below, with 5 meaning you strongly agree and 1 meaning you strongly disagree.

	Strongly Agree				Strongly Disagree
1. These MERIT program materials are applicable to my present duties.	5	4	3	2	1
2. The material presented in this module was personally helpful to me.	5	4	3	2	1
3. The program content was presented at a level that was easy to understand.	5	4	3	2	1
4. The program was organized in a way that was easy to follow.	5	4	3	2	1
5. The module exercises enhanced my learning of the material.	5	4	3	2	1
6. In general, the material presented in this module was new to me.	5	4	3	2	1
7. As a result of participating in this MERIT course, I anticipate some changes will come in the way I perform my job.	5	4	3	2	1
8. I would recommend this program to my co-workers.	5	4	3	2	1

Suggestions for improving the program and other comments:

_____

_____

_____

_____

_____

_____

_____

Thank you for participating in the Management Enrichment Training Program.
PLEASE RETURN THIS SHEET TO YOUR CREDIT UNION LEAGUE.